By the same author:

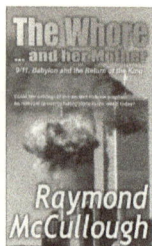

The Whore and her Mother
9/11, Babylon and the return of the king

Oh What Rapture!

Is a 'secret rapture' going to spare believers from tribulation to come?

#1 in the *Arrows* bible prophecy series

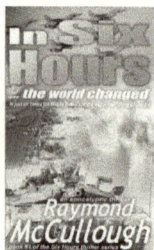

In Six Hours ...

the world changed

Apocalyptic fiction thriller

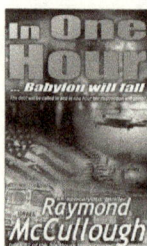

In One Hour ...

Babylon will fall

Apocalyptic fiction thriller – sequel

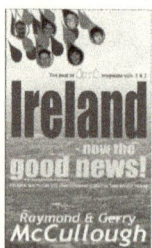

Ireland – now the good news!

The best of *'Bread'* – personal testimonies and church/fellowship profiles from around Ireland

Edited by *Raymond & Gerry McCullough*

Cover design: *Precious Oil Productions Ltd.*
Cover photos:

Israeli tank © Rafael Ben Ari – *dreamstime.com*

War devastation © Ded Mityay – *dreamstime.com*

Star of David © Anastasiia Kuznietsova – *dreamstime.com*

Neighbours from Hell

Israel and the coming nuclear attempt to destroy her

Raymond McCullough

Comments from other authors on _The Whore and her Mother:_

"… AMAZED when I read this book ... in awe of your extensive knowledge on so many levels: Christian, Jewish, and Muslim culture; the Jewish diaspora ... Greek & Hebrew; and your panoramic view of history through a biblical world view … thought-provoking and troublesome ... many will be offended, but you consistently build your case instead of being sensationalistic."

James Revoir, author of _Priceless Stones_

"… thoughtful, insightful ... and you have a knack for putting complicated topics in an easily accessible way."

Jim Darcy, author of _The Firelord's Crown_

".. has the makings of a best seller in its field ... you open up real ideas some of which are somewhat scary to say the least … difficult to leave down because you have created the 'Must turn the page' feeling threaded right through every line"

Colin T Mercer, UK, author & poet

"Love this kind of stuff ... grounded in research and common sense"
Francis Albert McGrath, Dublin, Ireland, author

"… most thought provoking ... meticulously researched and written with style and passion"

Sheila Belshaw, UK, author of _Pinpoint_

"It's very thought-provoking and solidly presented."
Katherine Holmes, author of _The Swan Bonnet_

"I did not feel you were preaching at all, more laying your cards on the table ... An evocative read, which left me 'thoughtful'"
Molly Hopkins, author of _It Happened in Paris_

"I was so impressed with the level of detail you give and your breadth of knowledge … well-researched and thorough"
Kevin Alex Baker, author of _Head Games_

Neighbours from Hell

Raymond McCullough

Published by

Precious Oil
PUBLICATIONS
www.preciousoil.com/publications

Precious Oil

PUBLICATIONS

www.preciousoil.com/publications

10a Listooder Road, Crossgar, Downpatrick, Northern Ireland BT30 9JE

Contents

Thanks to my wife, Gerry, for editing and general encouragement

Introduction

Several years ago, after publishing my first bible prophecy book, *'The Whore and her Mother,'* a close friend gave me a prophetic word. He shared a picture he had of me firing arrows. I believe it was a word of wisdom directing me to focus on one prophetic topic at a time – targeting it, as it were. Thus the *'Arrows bible prophecy series'* was birthed.

So far there are three books in the series: *'Oh What Rapture!,' 'Neighbours from Hell'* and *'Facing the Beast.'* This is the second book in the *Arrows* bible prophecy series and focusses on the coming war in the Middle East.

In 2015 I published *In Six Hours … the world changed* – a book of fiction based on the words of the Hebrew prophets. It covers the events of the prophesied *Six Hour War.* The 2019 sequel, *In One Hour … Babylon will fall,* covers the aftermath of that war and the prophesied ingathering of the Ten Tribes to a greatly expanded Israel.

Fiction is a great way to tell a story in a way that most people can relate to, but for those who desire to probe further and discover what the Hebrew prophets have actually foretold regarding these events, this short book is designed to provide that information. In other words, is there a scriptural foundation for what I have written?

Currently, *'the people of Israel have malicious neighbours who are painful briers and sharp thorns',* but in Ezekiel 28:24 we are told that will no longer be the case. Israel's neighbours have attacked the fledgeling state on numerous occasions – in 1948, 1967 and 1973 – with ongoing threats and intifadas in between.

Both Hezbollah, to the north, and Hamas, in the south west, have dedicated themselves to Israel's destruction. Their supposed *'peace partners'* in the Palestinian State continue to teach their children to hate Israel, to kill Jews, support those who do so, and long for the day when Israel no longer exists.

Syria is officially still at war with Israel and Iran continues to threaten her destruction. Turkey is using more and more aggressive language towards Israel. You could indeed say that Israel has *'neighbours from hell!'*

There are several prophets who spoke of these soon coming events – Moses, Isaiah, Jeremiah, Ezekiel, Obadiah, Zephaniah, Zechariah and Asaph, in the Book of Psalms. Their words dovetail to give us a fairly comprehensive picture of this coming war, which will transform the Middle East and affect the whole world.

Huge population transfers are involved – in Africa, Asia and the Middle East – incurring a tremendous worldwide refugee problem – and several nations which are currently found on a map of the Middle East will no longer exist! This war will have repercussions around the world – both politically and economically – and will affect future events.

It will be difficult for many to visualise these events – which is why I first wrote a fictional version – but, hopefully, anyone seeking after truth will find some satisfactory answers here. I've allowed a little conjecture within these pages – feel free to reject it! Hopefully, you will find the rest convincing – or at least worthy of prayerful consideration.

1 – Chaff in the wind ...

The Hebrew prophets; Isaiah, Asaph (the psalmist) and Zechariah tell us of a coming war in the Middle East, which has yet to take place. There are three main prophecies which deal with this – in Isaiah 17, Psalm 83 and Zechariah 12 – but further details are added in other prophecies.

Isaiah 17: A prophecy against Damascus:

'See, <u>Damascus will no longer be a city but will become a heap of ruins.</u> 2 The cities of Aroer will be deserted and left to flocks, which will lie down, with no one to make them afraid. 3 The fortified city will disappear from Ephraim, and royal power from Damascus; the remnant of Aram will be like the glory of the Israelites,' declares YHWH Almighty. 4 'In that day the glory of Jacob will fade; the fat of his body will waste away. 5 It will be as when reapers harvest the standing corn, gathering the corn in their arms – as when someone gleans ears of corn in the Valley of Rephaim. 6 Yet some gleanings will remain, as when an olive tree is beaten, leaving two or three olives on the topmost branches, four or five on the fruitful boughs,' declares YHWH, the God of Israel. 7 In that day people will look to their Maker and turn their eyes to the Holy One of Israel. 8 They will not look to the altars, the work of their hands, and they will have no regard for the Asherah poles and the incense altars their fingers have made. 9 In that day <u>their strong cities, which they left because of the Israelites, will be like places abandoned</u> to thickets and under-growth. And all will be desolation. 10 You have forgotten God your Saviour; you have not remembered the Rock, your fortress. Therefore, though you set out the finest plants and plant imported vines, 11 though on the day you set them out, you make them grow, and on the morning when you plant them, you bring them to bud, yet the harvest will be as nothing in the day of disease and incurable pain. 12 Woe to the <u>many nations that rage</u> – they rage like the raging sea! Woe to the peoples who roar – they roar like the roaring of great waters! 13 Although the peoples roar like the roar of surging waters, <u>when He rebukes them they flee far away, driven before the wind like chaff on the hills, like tumbleweed before a gale</u>. 14 <u>In the evening, sudden</u>

terror! Before the morning, they are gone! This is the portion of those who loot us, the lot of those who plunder us.

Isaiah 17 begins as a prophecy to one nation – Damascus and the other cities of Aram (i.e. modern day Syria) – but by verse 12 it becomes obvious that *'many nations'* are being referred to. These many nations are raging against Israel and then God promises his judgement against them – their cities will be abandoned and they will *'flee far away'*, and become *'like chaff on the hills, like tumbleweed before a gale.'*

Psalm 83: 1 O God, do not remain silent; do not turn a deaf ear, do not stand aloof, O God. 2 See how your enemies growl, how your foes rear their heads. 3 With cunning they conspire against your people; they plot against those you cherish. 4 'Come,' they say, 'let us destroy them as a nation, so that Israel's name is remembered no more.' 5 With one mind they plot together; they form an alliance against you – 6 the tents of Edom and the Ishmaelites, of Moab and the Hagrites, 7 Byblos [Gebal], Ammon and Amalek, Philistia, with the people of Tyre. 8 Even Assyria has joined them to reinforce Lot's descendants. 9 Do to them as you did to Midian, as you did to Sisera and Jabin at the River Kishon, 10 who perished at Endor and became like dung on the ground. 11 Make their nobles like Oreb and Zeeb, all their princes like Zebah and Zalmunna, 12 who said, 'Let us take possession of the pasture-lands of God.' 13 Make them like tumbleweed, my God, like chaff before the wind. 14 As fire consumes the forest or a flame sets the mountains ablaze, 15 so pursue them with your tempest and terrify them with your storm. 16 Cover their faces with shame, Lord, so that they will seek Your name. 17 May they ever be ashamed and dismayed; may they perish in disgrace. 18 Let them know that You, whose name is YHWH – that You alone are the Most High over all the earth.

In this psalm Asaph adds to the dramatic picture: *"As fire consumes the forest or a flame sets the mountains ablaze so pursue them with your tempest and terrify them with your storm"*, he says.

2 Chronicles 29:30 King Hezekiah and his officials ordered the Levites to praise YHWH with the words of David and of Asaph the seer.

Asaph is declared to be a prophet – not just a psalmist!

Isaiah also shows that the attack will be sudden, without warning, and that the threat will only be of short duration (v.14) – *"in the evening sudden terror! Before the morning, they are gone!"* That is why I have coined the phrase – *'Six Hour War'* – when referring to this conflict.

It will be a short, overnight, existential threat to the nation of Israel, but by morning the tables will have turned so much that the attacking nations will flee away – and Israel will pursue them! This will be a conflict similar in nature to the Six Day War of 1967, but will turn even more dramatically in favour of Israel – hence the phrase, *'Six Hour War'.*

Psalm 83 uses very similar language to that of Isaiah – *"make them like tumbleweed, my God, like chaff before the wind"* – but is specific about the nations who will be involved in this attack.

Who are these nations who will attack Israel?

> The tents of Edom, the Ishmaelites,
> Moab and the Hagrites,
> Byblos (Gebal), Ammon, Amalek,
> Philistia,
> the people of Tyre,
> Assyria has joined with them.

Aram and Damascus we have already identified as **Syria**. Edom were the descendants of Israel's brother, Esau, and lived to the east and south of Israel – roughly corresponding to southern Jordan and NE **Saudi Arabia** today (more careful identification of the Edomites in chapter 11).

The Ishmaelites are the descendants of Abraham's eldest son, Ishmael, who moved to the east into Arabia – what is now Saudi Arabia today. The Moabites and Ammonites were the descendants of Abraham's nephew, Lot. They became implacable enemies of Israel and would correspond to the modern day country of **Jordan** (more in chapter 6).

The Hagrites lived in Gilead and to the east – possibly the south of Syria today. The Amalekites lived to the south of Israel – roughly the Sinai peninsula today (Egypt). The people of Tyre and Byblos refer to cities which are today part of the **Lebanon**. Philistia is included – corresponding to the Gaza Strip particularly (where the Philistines once lived) – but also to **Palestinians** in general.

Finally, the Assyrians are referred to as having *'joined with them, to reinforce Lot's descendants'*, which would seem to mean that Iraq – and probably, Iran (a non-Arab nation) – will join with these other nations (all of them Arab).

This is a very brief look at who will perform this attack – a more detailed identification is undertaken in *Chapters 6-14 – Meet the Neighbours*.

Another major non-Arab Islamic country in the area that is specifically NOT included is Turkey – so we will assume that Turkey will keep out of this conflict.

So who do we have then? – Lebanon, Syria, Jordan, Iraq, Saudi Arabia and most likely Egypt (including the ISIS-linked forces in the Sinai) – countries immediately bordering on the present-day State of Israel – probably joined by Iran (a country that aspires to nuclear power!). This certainly sounds like a recipe for trouble – especially if you happen to live in Israel!

The prophet Zechariah also adds to our knowledge of this coming war.

Zechariah 12: 1-9 A prophecy: the word of YHWH concerning Israel.

1 YHWH, who stretches out the heavens, who lays the foundation of the earth, and who forms the human spirit within a person, declares: 2 'I am going to make Jerusalem <u>a cup that sends all the surrounding peoples reeling</u>. Judah will be besieged as well as Jerusalem. 3 On that day, when all the nations of the earth are gathered against her, I will make Jerusalem an immovable rock for all the nations. All who try to move it will injure themselves. 4 On that day I will strike every horse with panic and its rider with madness,' declares YHWH. 'I will keep a watchful eye over Judah, but I will blind all the horses of the nations. 5 Then the clans of Judah will say in their hearts, "The people of Jerusalem are strong, because YHWH Almighty is their God." 6 'On that day I will make the clans of Judah like a brazier in a woodpile, like a flaming torch among sheaves. <u>They will consume all the surrounding peoples right and left</u>, but Jerusalem will remain intact in her place. 7 'YHWH will save the dwellings of Judah first, so that the honour of the house of David and of Jerusalem's inhabitants may not be greater than that of Judah. 8 On that day YHWH will shield those who live in Jerusalem, so that the feeblest among them will be like David, and the house of David will be like God, like the angel

of YHWH going before them. 9 On that day <u>I will set out to destroy all the nations that attack Jerusalem</u>.

Zechariah adds to Asaph's similes to describe what he will do to the *'surrounding peoples'* – Israel will be *"like a brazier in a woodpile, like a flaming torch among sheaves. They will consume all the surrounding peoples right and left"* – *"a cup that sends all the surrounding peoples reeling."*

So, this attack will come upon Israel without warning, with a serious threat of Israel's annihilation, but will turn around very suddenly in Israel's favour (between evening and before morning – ie. about six hours, give or take). Israel will suddenly arise as a fierce opponent – *"the feeblest among them will be like David"*, consuming all the surrounding peoples and destroying them.

The prophet Micah again adds to the story:

Micah 4:11 But now <u>many nations are gathered against you. They say, "Let her be defiled, let our eyes gloat over Zion!"</u> 12 But they do not know the thoughts of YHWH; they do not understand his plan, that he has gathered them like sheaves to the threshing floor. 13 "Rise and thresh, Daughter Zion, for I will give you horns of iron; I will give you hooves of bronze, and <u>you will break to pieces many nations." You will devote their ill-gotten gains to YHWH, their wealth to YHWH of all the earth</u>.

Micah refers to *'many nations'* being gathered against Israel, gloating over her. Israel, he says, will thresh them like sheaves – *'you will break to pieces many nations.'* He also refers to Israel gaining control of the wealth of those nations!

Ezekiel also adds to the story, in chapter 28 – a prophecy not just specifically to the nation of Lebanon (Sidon), but also referring to *'all their neighbours'*:

Ezekiel 28 <u>A prophecy against Sidon</u>

20 The word of YHWH came to me: 21 'Son of man, set your face against Sidon; prophesy against her 22 and say: "This is what the Sovereign Lord says: "'I am against you, Sidon, and among you I will display my glory. You will know that I am YHWH, when I inflict punishment on you and within you am proved to be holy. 23 I will send a plague upon you and make blood flow in your streets. The slain will fall within you, with the sword against you on every side. Then you will know that I am YHWH. 24 "'No

<u>longer will the people of Israel have malicious neighbours who are painful briers and sharp thorns</u>. Then they will know that I am the Sovereign YHWH. 25 "'This is what the Sovereign YHWH says: when I gather the people of Israel from the nations where they have been scattered, I will be proved holy through them in the sight of the nations. Then they will live in their own land, which I gave to my servant Jacob. 26 They will live there in safety and will build houses and plant vineyards; <u>they will live in safety when I inflict punishment on all their neighbours who maligned them</u>. Then they will know that I am YHWH their God.'"

Who do we know who are currently *'malicious neighbours'* of Israel, living in Sidon (Lebanon) and acting as *'painful briers and sharp thorns'* towards Israel? Hezbollah! Through Ezekiel God is promising to inflict punishment on these people!

The timing of the fulfilment of this prophecy is indicated in verse 25 – *'when I gather the people of Israel from the nations where they have been scattered'*. That description has only been relevant since the restoration of the State of Israel in 1948. Ezekiel says *'Israel will no longer have malicious neighbours who are painful briers and sharp thorns'*.

Currently, Israel's neighbours include the Palestinians – both Hamas in Gaza and the PLO/Fatah in Judea and Samaria; Hezbollah, both in Lebanon and Syria, and the Iranians, and others such as Al Nusra, in Syria. There are also elements of ISIS in the Sinai. All of these are thorns in the side of Israel – at present – but Ezekiel says a day is coming when that will no longer be the case.

This will be a very different Middle East after this war. The rest of the world will have been completely taken by surprise and will be faced, presumably, with a massive refugee problem. And the countries involved – destroyed in this conflict – will be not only the nations immediately surrounding Israel – Syria, Lebanon, Iraq, Jordan, Saudi Arabia, Egypt – but will also include Iran, a substantial nation of around 75 million people!

The *Six Hour War* – summary:

1. Israel will be attacked by the nations immediately surrounding her – intent *'that Israel's name is remembered no more'.* The attack will begin in the evening, but the threat to Israel will be gone before morning.

2. The attacking nations – Syria, Jordan, Lebanon, Egypt, Saudi Arabia and Iran (and probably Iraq and Sudan) – will *'flee far away'* from Israel, who will *'send them reeling'*, *'consuming them right and left'*. The thorns in their side – Hamas, Fatah, Hezbollah, ISIS, Al Nusrah, Iran – all gone!

3. *'Their strong cities ...will be abandoned'* – Israel will inherit their land and resources.

4. Israel will be able to live in safety and security, not having to regularly defend herself against terrorism.

2 – The destruction of Elam

The nation of Iran is a major player in the world today, but the prophet Jeremiah gave a word concerning Elam, (i.e. Iran).

Jeremiah 49 A message about Elam

34 This is the word of YHWH that came to Jeremiah the prophet concerning Elam, early in the reign of Zedekiah king of Judah: 35 This is what YHWH Almighty says: 'See, I will break the bow of Elam, the mainstay of their might. 36 I will bring against Elam the four winds from the four quarters of heaven; <u>I will scatter them to the four winds, and there will not be a nation where Elam's exiles do not go</u>. 37 <u>I will shatter Elam</u> before their foes, before those who want to kill them; <u>I will bring disaster on them</u>, even my fierce anger,' declares YHWH. 'I will pursue them with the sword until I have made an end of them. 38 <u>I will set my throne in Elam</u> and destroy her king and officials,' declares YHWH. 39 'Yet I will restore the fortunes of Elam in days to come,' declares YHWH.

A nation of 75 million people will be *"scattered to the four winds"*, says YHWH through Jeremiah, *"and there will not be a nation where Elam's exiles do not go."* This is complete destruction – something which to date has never happened to the nation of Persia/Iran. Certainly they have been conquered – by Alexander the Great, for instance – and become subservient to other nations, but they have never been destroyed and sent into exile in the way Jeremiah describes in this prophecy.

Why would YHWH decide to destroy the nation of Iran? Why would he send them into exile all across the earth? Because they plotted, along with their Arab allies – the traditional enemies of Israel – to totally wipe out the nation of Israel, to remove Israel from the map!

What does it mean that YHWH will set his throne in Elam? Presumably, that Israel will gain control of the territory of the devastated nation, in order to facilitate the coming ingathering of the ten tribes of Israel. In the following chapter I have a couple of suggestions as to how this might come about.

It is an interesting fact that the underground Christian church in Iran today is the fastest growing church in the world – despite being under a hostile Islamic dictatorship. And the members of that church are praying for the present-day fulfilment of Jeremiah's prophecy – so that they can carry the gospel with them to every corner of the world.

Destruction of Elam (Iran) – summary:

1. Iran – a nation of 75 million – will be destroyed and *'scattered to the four winds'*.

2. Refugees from Iran will travel to every nation – *'there will not be a nation where Elam's exiles do not go.'*

3. Iran will no longer be a barrier to the ingathering of the Ten Tribes from Asia – the highway to Assyria will be open.

3 – A nuclear attack?

The prophet Zechariah gives a very unusual prophecy in chapter 5:

Zechariah 5:1 I looked again, and there before me was a flying scroll. 2 He asked me, 'What do you see?' I answered, 'I see a flying scroll, twenty cubits long and ten cubits wide.' 3 And he said to me, 'This is the curse that is going out over the whole land; for according to what it says on one side, every thief will be banished, and according to what it says on the other, everyone who swears falsely will be banished. 4 YHWH Almighty declares, "I will send it out, and it will enter the house of the thief and the house of anyone who swears falsely by my name. It will remain in that house and destroy it completely, both its timbers and its stones."'

5 Then the angel who was speaking to me came forward and said to me, 'Look up and see what is appearing.' 6 I asked, 'What is it?' He replied, 'It is a basket.' And he added, 'This is the iniquity of the people throughout the land.' 7 Then the cover of lead was raised, and there in the basket sat a woman [alt: fire]! 8 He said, 'This is wickedness,' and he pushed her [it] back into the basket and pushed its lead cover down on it.

9 Then I looked up – and there before me were two women, with the wind in their wings! They had wings like those of a stork, and they lifted up the basket between heaven and earth. 10 'Where are they taking the basket?' I asked the angel who was speaking to me. 11 He replied, 'To the country of Babylonia [Shinar] to build a house for it. When the house is ready, the basket will be set there in its place.'

Zechariah 5 contains what appear to be two very strange prophecies. The first four verses refer to a flying scroll – in other words, a cylinder. A royal cubit is 20.61 inches, so the dimensions of this scroll are 34.35 feet long and about 17 feet wide – this is a huge cylinder! Now, to get a better understanding we need to realise that Hebrew writers in those days did not have a concept of diameter, but measured the circumference instead.

So, if we take the second dimension to mean the circumference, we are dealing with a cylinder that is 34.35 feet long and about 5.47 feet in diameter – ie. 10.47m x 1.67m.

This flying scroll/cylinder contains a curse. The description is of something capable of destroying a house – not only the wood, but the stones also. It is also described as <u>remaining</u> in the house – perhaps referring to the radiation fallout? Could this actually be a reference to a nuclear missile?

Let's examine the second prophecy – in verses 5-11. It refers to an *ephah* – Hebrew for a basket, or container – often used as a measure. This container apparently has a woman inside? That doesn't make a great deal of sense, unless we examine the alternative meaning of the Hebrew word *ishshah,* (usually translated in this passage as *'woman'*) – but in other parts of the Old Testament the same word is translated as a *'fire offering'*, (eg. in Exodus 29:18,25), which would seem to make much more sense in the context.

So, instead we have a cylindrical container, with fire inside, which has a lead covering, or lid. Lead is used to shield a nuclear device so that harmful radiation is not emitted. The cylinder is described as *'flying'* and in verse 9 there is mention of *'wings like those of a stork'*, which *'lifted the container up between heaven and earth'*.

Combining this description of the contents with the earlier one of the container itself, we have a pretty good description of a typical nuclear ballistic missile!

Finally (verse 11), we are given the location of these missiles – *'to the country of Shinar, to build a house for it. When the house is ready, the basket will be set there in its place.'*

Shinar is within the borders of modern day Iran, so the missiles described here will apparently be stored in prepared bases – silos – in Iran until they are put to use against Israel in the *Six Hour War,* with the intention of *'wiping Israel off the map!'*

The *Six Hour War* involves Iran, plus the nations surrounding Israel – most of whom do not possess nuclear missiles – so this will be an initial nuclear attack, followed by an all-out conventional war against Israel. The outcome, however, will not be as these nations planned – Israel will turn the tables and devour the nations around them.

How will this come about? I don't know for sure – this will be the hand of YHWH in action – but I *can* make a couple of suggestions.

First, Israelis have been involved for many years in the design of sophisticated computer systems, they have been at the forefront of many developments in software used around the world. This includes the software used to guide missiles – both nuclear and conventional.

Is it conceivable that they would not leave themselves access to software that might be one day be used against them? Israel have a very advanced cyber-warfare unit and have quite possibly infiltrated the missile control software of Iran, Syria, Saudi Arabia, Egypt, etc.

I suspect they may have infiltrated this software in a way similar to that in which *Iron Dome* operates – i.e. it would take no action if a weapon is aimed at a target other than Israel, but would take action to re-direct the missile if it is targeted on an Israeli city. This re-direction could return the missile to sender, or divert it to a nearby enemy city. Either way the aggression would not be initiated by Israel – simply diverted from the intended target.

Secondly, we should not assume that Saudi Arabia do not have access to nuclear missiles. This nation is currently involved in a proxy war with Iran in Yemen and has a close relationship with fellow Sunni nation, Pakistan – who undoubtedly DO have nuclear missiles. Saudi Arabia may already have Pakistani nuclear missiles stockpiled as a last resort to use against Iran.

In the event of a perceived nuclear attack from Iran (something all too possible in the heat and confusion of a war), Saudi Arabia could retaliate against Iran with these weapons – resulting in what could easily become a devastating nuclear war between Iran and Saudi Arabia, with both nations (and possibly Iraq, also) reduced to a smoking ruin!

This would leave Iran – and possibly Iraq – uninhabitable and the way open for many millions of the ten tribes to travel through that land on their way home to Israel.

<u>Nuclear attack? – summary:</u>

1. Zechariah describes a cylinder of dimensions similar to many of today's nuclear missiles.

2. The cylinder/container contains fire (a curse) that can destroy both wood and stone, yet *'remains'* – and is carried on wings between earth and heaven (upper atmosphere).

3. The container is placed in a *'house'* – base – in the land of Shinar (Iran), ready to be used against Israel.

4 – Then they will know

The intention of the *Six Hour War* – as far as her enemies are concerned – will be to destroy Israel once and for all – to *'wipe Israel off the map'!* But that is certainly not God's intention: *'Indeed, he who watches over Israel will neither slumber nor sleep'.* (**Psalm 121:4**)

YHWH's hand of protection is over Israel and will continue to be over Israel. The outcome of this war will be very different from the intention of Israel's enemies – in fact, the consequences for them will be nothing short of disastrous!

Then they will know that I AM YHWH!

Isaiah 17:7 In that day people will look to their Maker and turn their eyes to the Holy One of Israel. 8 They will not look to the altars, the work of their hands, and they will have no regard for the Asherah poles and the incense altars their fingers have made. 10 You have forgotten God your Saviour; you have not remembered the Rock, your fortress.

Syria (Damascus) *'will look to … the Holy One of Israel.'*

Psalm 83:18 Let them know that you, whose name is YHWH – that you alone are the Most High over all the earth.

Ezekiel 28 (specifically to Tyre and Sidon = Lebanon)

23 Then you will know that I am YHWH.

24 Then they will know that I am the Sovereign YHWH.

25 This is what the Sovereign YHWH says: when I gather the people of Israel from the nations where they have been scattered, I will be proved holy through them in the sight of the nations. Then they will live in their own land, which I gave to my servant Jacob. 26 They will live there in safety and will build houses and plant vineyards; they will live in safety when I inflict punishment on all their neighbours who maligned them. Then they will know that I am YHWH their God."

Not only Lebanon (Tyre and Sidon), but *'all their neighbours … will know that I am YHWH their God.'*

Ezekiel 25 A prophecy against Philistia (Gaza)

15 'This is what the Sovereign YHWH says: "Because the Philistines acted in vengeance and took revenge with malice in their hearts, and with ancient hostility sought to destroy Judah, 16 therefore this is what the Sovereign YHWH says: I am about to stretch out my hand against the Philistines, and I will wipe out the Kerethites and destroy those remaining along the coast. 17 I will carry out great vengeance on them and punish them in my wrath. Then they will know that I am YHWH, when I take vengeance on them."'

Gaza (Philistia) *'will know that I am YHWH.'*

Ezekiel 25:21 So YHWH will make himself known to the Egyptians, and in that day they will acknowledge YHWH. They will worship with sacrifices and grain offerings; they will make vows to YHWH and keep them. 22 YHWH will strike Egypt with a plague; he will strike them and heal them. They will turn to YHWH, and he will respond to their pleas and heal them.

'The Egyptians … will acknowledge YHWH. They will worship … they will make vows to YHWH and keep them … They will turn to YHWH.'

Syria, Lebanon, Gaza, Egypt – *'all* [Israel's] *neighbours … will know that I am YHWH.'*

This war has an explicit purpose – beyond Israel being victorious in it and her subsequent expansion and control of the Middle East. That purpose is the salvation of the peoples of those lands surrounding Israel – currently dominated by Islam – that they may know that YHWH is the only true God and come to know Him. Another way of putting this same statement is that they will know that Allah is NOT God! Confidence in Islam will have been shattered!

Unfortunately, the leaders, rulers and ayatollahs of the Muslim world tend to respect only one thing – strength. They remain unimpressed by western democracy – which is derived from Christianity – seeing only weakness in it and believing that they will ultimately undermine and overcome it.

However, the victory of the tiny nation of Israel – standing alone against the might of the surrounding Arab nations, allied with

Iran – will surely cause a great humiliation to the pride and power of Islam. Such a defeat, giving control to Israel of all the wealth and power of the Middle East – Iran no longer being even a nation, but now a scattering of exiles, just as the Jews were for almost two millennia – will surely cause many Muslims to question their trust in Mohammed and his God, Allah.

The Christian world should be ready and prepared to satisfy a sudden great hunger among Arabs and other Muslims for knowledge of the Judaeo-Christian God, YHWH. Are we preparing for this with material written in Arabic, Persian, etc. – explaining who YHWH is and his son, *Issa al Masih* (Yeshuah/Jesus, the Messiah)? I doubt it!

Then they will know – summary:

1. *'In that day people will look to their Maker and turn their eyes to the Holy One of Israel.'* The outcome of this war will be that the Arab nations will turn to YHWH.

2. Over and over He says, *'that they may know that I am YHWH'* – to Syria, to Lebanon, to Gaza, to Egypt and to all that attack (Psalm 83:18)

3. Another way of putting this is *'they will know that Allah is not God!'* Israel's defeat of a greatly superior force will cause Muslims to lose confidence in Allah and turn to YHWH – especially in Egypt.

4. Are we preparing for this great revival in former Arab countries and among the refugees from this war? No, I didn't think so!

5 – The Ingathering

A secondary, but also very important, purpose of this war will be to clear the way so that the ten tribes may return – the Ingathering. Modern Israel is composed almost entirely of the tribes of Judah and Benjamin, with a scattering from the tribe of Levi – two and a half tribes, if you like.

Isaiah 32:12 Beat your breasts for the pleasant fields, for the fruitful vines 13 and for <u>the land of my people, a land overgrown with thorns and briers</u> – yes, mourn for all houses of merriment and for this city of revelry. 14 The fortress will be abandoned, the noisy city deserted; citadel and watchtower <u>will become a wasteland for ever</u>, the delight of donkeys, a pasture for flocks, 15 <u>till the Spirit is poured on us from on high, and the desert becomes a fertile field, and the fertile field seems like a forest</u>. 16 YHWH's justice will dwell in the desert, his righteousness live in the fertile field. 17 The fruit of that righteous-ness will be peace; its effect will be quietness and confidence for ever. 18 <u>My people will live in peaceful dwelling-places, in secure homes, in undisturbed places of rest</u>. 19 Though hail flattens the forest and the city is levelled completely, 20 how blessed you will be, sowing your seed by every stream, and letting your cattle and donkeys range free.

In the past, before the Jews began to return to the land, it was described by those few travellers who visited it as a wasteland – a place of malarial swamps, thorns and briers. Mark Twain visited the Holy Land in 1867 and wrote letters for his paper, the *Alta California*, in which he said:

'Of all the lands there are for <u>dismal scenery</u>, I think Palestine must be the prince. The hills are barren, they are dull of color, they are unpicturesque in shape. The valleys are unsightly deserts fringed with a feeble vegetation that has an expression about it of being sorrowful and despondent.'

Later, in his subsequent book, *The Innocents Abroad*, he wrote:

'The further we went the hotter the sun got, and the more rocky and bare, repulsive and dreary the landscape became ... There was hardly a tree or a shrub anywhere. Even the olive and the cactus, those fast friends of a worthless soil, had almost deserted the country.'

Twain was obviously not impressed! But Isaiah prophesied; *'the desert becomes a fertile field, and the fertile field seems like a forest'* – which has already been fulfilled in Israel today. He goes on to say, *'My people will live in peaceful dwelling-places, in secure homes, in undisturbed places of rest.'* This is NOT the case at present, but *will* be the outcome of the *Six Hour War.*

If I were to include all of the prophecies of the people of Israel returning to the land (*eretz*) this would be an extremely long chapter – though I'd recommend a study of it. Let's just take a couple of examples:

Isaiah 11:11 In that day YHWH will reach out his hand a second time to reclaim the surviving remnant of his people from Assyria, from Lower Egypt, from Upper Egypt, from Cush, from Elam, from Babylonia, from Hamath and from the islands of the Mediterranean. 12 He will raise a banner for the nations and gather the exiles of Israel; he will assemble the scattered people of Judah from the four quarters of the earth. 13 Ephraim's jealousy will vanish, and Judah's enemies will be destroyed; Ephraim will not be jealous of Judah, nor Judah hostile towards Ephraim.14 They will swoop down on the slopes of Philistia to the west; together they will plunder the people to the east. They will subdue Edom and Moab, and the Ammonites will be subject to them.

The references to Ephraim and Judah represent the two separated groups of Israelites – Judah: the Jews, still scattered around the world, although nearly half are now living in Israel; and Ephraim, representing the other ten tribes – also scattered around the world. The jealousy and hostility (*harass*-ment in some translations) referred to may relate to the difficulty some of the ten tribe nations have had in trying to make *aliyah* to Israel.

The Israeli Interior Ministry have not made this easy – especially for groups from Africa and Asia, i.e. Israelites who are not white-skinned. For instance, *aliyah* of the Menashe tribe (Manasseh – from eastern India and Myanmar) – to Israel is being restricted to only 100 per year. More than 25,000 have applied to make *aliyah*, so, at the present rate, it will take 250 years to get them all home!

And that's only those who have already converted to orthodox Judaism! There are a total of around four million Menashe – most of them Christian – you can see the problem! Obviously, something will have to give in terms of Israeli bureaucracy and attitudes. Judah will have to *'stop harassing Ephraim'.*

The valley of dry bones and the two sticks

Ezekiel 37 The valley of dry bones

1 The hand of YHWH was on me, and he brought me out by the Spirit of YHWH and set me in the middle of a valley; it was full of bones. 2 He led me to and fro among them, and I saw a great many bones on the floor of the valley, bones that were very dry. 3 He asked me, 'Son of man, can these bones live?' I said, 'Sovereign YHWH, you alone know.'

4 Then he said to me, 'Prophesy to these bones and say to them, "Dry bones, hear the word of the Lord! 5 This is what the Sovereign YHWH says to these bones: I will make breath enter you, and you will come to life. 6 I will attach tendons to you and make flesh come upon you and cover you with skin; I will put breath in you, and you will come to life. Then you will know that I am YHWH.'"

7 So I prophesied as I was commanded. And as I was prophesying, there was a noise, a rattling sound, and the bones came together, bone to bone. 8 I looked, and tendons and flesh appeared on them and skin covered them, but there was no breath in them.

9 Then he said to me, 'Prophesy to the breath; prophesy, son of man, and say to it, "This is what the Sovereign YHWH says: come, breath, from the four winds and breathe into these slain, that they may live."' 10 So I prophesied as he commanded me, and breath entered them; they came to life and stood up on their feet – a vast army.

11 Then he said to me: 'Son of man, <u>these bones are the people of Israel. They say, "Our bones are dried up and our hope is gone; we are cut off."</u> 12 Therefore prophesy and say to them: "This is what the Sovereign YHWH says: my people, <u>I am going to open your graves and bring you up from them; I will bring you back to the land of Israel</u>. 13 Then you, my people, will know that I am YHWH, when I open your graves and bring you up from them. 14 <u>I will put my Spirit in you and you will live, and I will settle you in your own land</u>. Then you will know that I YHWH have spoken, and I have done it, declares YHWH.'"

Chapter 5 – The Ingathering

15 The word of YHWH came to me: 16 'Son of man, take a stick of wood and write on it, "Belonging to Judah and the Israelites associated with him." Then take another stick of wood, and write on it, "Belonging to Joseph (that is, to Ephraim) and all the Israelites associated with him." 17 Join them to-gether into one stick so that they will become one in your hand.

18 'When your people ask you, "Won't you tell us what you mean by this?" 19 say to them, "This is what the Sovereign YHWH says: <u>I am going to take the stick of Joseph</u> – which is in Ephraim's hand – <u>and of the Israelite tribes associated with him, and join it to Judah's stick. I will make them into a single stick of wood, and they will become one in my hand</u>." 20 Hold before their eyes the sticks you have written on 21 and say to them, "This is what the Sovereign YHWH says: <u>I will take the Israelites out of the nations where they have gone. I will gather them from all around and bring them back into their own land. 22 I will make them one nation in the land, on the mountains of Israel</u>. There will be one king over all of them and <u>they will never again be two nations or be divided into two kingdoms</u>.

The ten tribes today are *'cut off'* from Israel – partly because of Israeli bureaucracy, but mainly because of both geographical and monetary reasons. Imagine the cost of flying 100 million people to Israel from Asia and Africa – not economically feasible.

The alternative is to travel there overland and that is the geographical problem: the way is not open because there are extremely hostile nations in the way – Iran and Iraq on the Asian side and Egypt and Sudan on the African side. But YHWH says, *'I will bring you back to the land of Israel'* and *'you will live, and I will settle you in your own land.'* So, it *will* happen.

The second part of Ezekiel's prophecy concerns the two sticks – one for Judah *'and the Israelites associated with him'*; one for Joseph *'and all the Israelites associated with him.'* Judah – the Jews – includes Benjamin and many from the tribe of Levi; Joseph (Ephraim) includes all the remaining ten tribes, including more from Levi. They will be joined together *'and they will never again be two nations or be divided into two kingdoms.'*

When this happens it will, I believe, be one of the most amazing miracles of all time – one hundred million people travelling thousands of miles to return to *'their land'* after so many hundreds of years of exile. Only YHWH could achieve this.

The so-called *'lost'* ten tribes of Israel are really not difficult to find in many parts of the earth today. But there are two areas in the world that hold a particularly high concentration of Israelites – in Asia and Africa – specifically, the Pashtuns in Asia (Pakistan, Afghanistan and in parts of India) and the Igbo in southern Nigeria.

There are also the Menashe in India/Myanmar, Kashmiris in India/Pakistan, the Lemba in South Africa/Zimbabwe, Tutsi in Rwanda – plus some interesting evidence of Israelite origin in the Japanese people!*

The Highway

Again, these two areas – Egypt and Assyria – are referred to in prophecy:

Isaiah 11:15 YHWH will dry up the gulf of the Egyptian sea; with a scorching wind he will sweep his hand over the <u>River Euphrates. He will break it up into seven streams so that anyone can cross over in sandals</u>. 16 There will be a <u>highway for the remnant of his people that is left from Assyria</u>, as there was for Israel when they came up from Egypt.

Isaiah 19 16 In that day the Egyptians will become weaklings. They will shudder with fear at the uplifted hand that YHWH Almighty raises against them. 17 And <u>the land of Judah will bring terror to the Egyptians; everyone to whom Judah is mentioned will be terrified</u>, because of what YHWH Almighty is planning against them.

23 <u>In that day there will be a highway from Egypt to Assyria. The Assyrians will go to Egypt and the Egyptians to Assyria</u>. The Egyptians and Assyrians will worship together. 24 In that day Israel will be the third, along with Egypt and Assyria, a blessing on the earth. 25 YHWH Almighty will bless them, saying, 'Blessed be Egypt my people, Assyria my handiwork, and Israel my inheritance.'

Isaiah 27:13 <u>Those who were perishing in Assyria and those who were exiled in Egypt will come and worship YHWH</u> on the holy mountain in Jerusalem.

---

* see Bibliography

Micah 7:11 The day for building your walls will come, the day for extending your boundaries. 12 <u>In that day people will come to you from Assyria and the cities of Egypt, even from Egypt to the Euphrates</u> and from sea to sea and from mountain to mountain.

There will be a highway from Egypt to Assyria – through Israel! This doesn't just refer to a modern road leading from A to B – that exists already – but to a specific route used in a particular way, an *'open road'*. In this case the highway is *'for the remnant of* [YHWH's] *people that is left from Assyria'* (**Isaiah 11:15**) and will be used by the exiled ten tribes returning home to the land of Israel – via Assyria, and Egypt! *'In that day people will come to you from Assyria and the cities of Egypt … from Egypt to the Euphrates'.'* (**Micah 7:12**)

If the Igbo people (around 40 million of them!) and other Israelite tribes in Africa – the Lemba in South Africa/Zimbabwe; the Tutsi, in Rwanda/Burundi – wished to return by land to Israel, they would currently find their way blocked by the hostile nations of Egypt and Sudan (a nation once joined with Egypt and so possibly included with Egypt in these prophecies).

Before these tribes can contemplate returning to Israel this obstacle needs to be removed. Isaiah, in Chapter 19, says that the terror of Israel will fall on the Egyptians – they *"will become weaklings"* and *"shudder with fear"* – and that there will be a highway there. In other words the way will become open, immigration to Israel will become a possibility!

Even the *'gulf of the Egyptian Sea'* (Gulf of Suez?) will be dried up to facilitate this aliyah – as will also the great river Euphrates *'break up into seven streams – so that anyone can cross over in sandals'*. But this is not just for anyone, it is specifically for the people of Israel – *'<u>there will be a highway for the remnant of His people</u> that is left from Assyria.'* (**Isaiah 11**)

The Pashtuns (more than 50 million of them – 33 million in Pakistan, 15 million in Afghanistan and another 3 million in India[*]) and other Israelite tribes in Asia – such as the Menashe, in India/Myanmar (4 million); and the Kashmiris (7 million) in India/Pakistan – are currently unable to travel to Israel through a

---

[*] https://en.wikipedia.org/wiki/Pashtuns

hostile Iran/Iraq. But, according to Jeremiah 49 (see last chapter), Iran will be in exile after the *Six Hour War* – so now the way will also be open for the tribes from Asia to return, the highway from Assyria!

Currently, the mighty Shatt-Al-Arab waterway – the joining together of two great rivers, the Tigris and the Euphrates, which flows through the city of Basra in Iraq – does not have even one proper bridge! Since the Gulf War in 1991 there are a total of three temporary pontoon bridges across this great waterway. It will clearly be an obstacle to the return of the tribes from Asia/Assyria.

However, if the river dries up into seven streams – as prophesied by Isaiah – it will be possible to build several temporary crossing places to facilitate the huge aliyah of God's people from Pakistan, Afghanistan and beyond.

Greater Israel

The concept of *'a greater Israel'* is usually frowned upon today – being seen as a right wing and extremist idea and not politically correct! However, the concept originates in the prophetic scriptures. The boundaries of Israel were defined right back in Genesis and repeated again in Deuteronomy.

Genesis 15:18 On that day YHWH made a covenant with Abram and said, 'To your descendants I give this land, from the Wadi of Egypt to the great river, the Euphrates – 19 the land of the Kenites, Kenizzites, Kadmonites, 20 Hittites, Perizzites, Rephaites, 21 Amorites, Canaanites, Girgashites and Jebusites.'

Deuteronomy 1:6 YHWH our God said to us at Horeb, 'You have stayed long enough at this mountain. 7 Break camp and advance into the hill country of the Amorites; go to all the neighbouring peoples in the Arabah, in the mountains, in the western foothills, in the Negev and along the coast, to the land of the Canaanites and to Lebanon, as far as the great river, the Euphrates. 8 See, I have given you this land. Go in and take possession of the land that YHWH swore he would give to your fathers – to Abraham, Isaac and Jacob – and to their descendants after them.'

Deuteronomy 11:24 Every place where you set your foot will be yours: your territory will extend from the desert to Lebanon, and from the River Euphrates to the Mediterranean Sea. 25 No one will be able to stand against you. <u>YHWH your God, as he promised you, will put the terror and fear of you on the whole land,</u> wherever you go.

Isaiah 27:12 In that day YHWH will thresh <u>from the flowing Euphrates to the Wadi of Egypt,</u> and you, Israel, will be gathered up one by one. 13 And in that day a great trumpet will sound. <u>Those who were perishing in Assyria and those who were exiled in Egypt will come and worship YHWH</u> on the holy mountain in Jerusalem.

The boundaries of *'greater Israel'* are from the *'brook of Egypt'* (usually taken to be Wadi El-Arish in the Sinai) to the River Euphrates, and includes all of Lebanon and certainly the Golan area – formerly known as the land of Gilead and Bashan, where the three tribes of Reuben, Gad and Manasseh received their inheritance from Moses, on the other side of the Jordan.

The future land of Israel is referred to in Isaiah 49, where the return of the exiled tribes is referred to:

Isaiah 49 17 Your children hasten back, and <u>those who laid you waste depart from you.</u> 18 Lift up your eyes and look around; <u>all your children gather and come to you.</u> As surely as I live,' declares YHWH, 'you will wear them all as ornaments; you will put them on, like a bride. 19 'Though you were ruined and made desolate and your land laid waste, <u>now you will be too small for your people,</u> and <u>those who devoured you will be far away.</u> 20 The children born during your bereavement will yet say in your hearing, "<u>This place is too small for us; give us more space to live in.</u>" 21 Then you will say in your heart, "Who bore me these? I was bereaved and barren; I was exiled and rejected. Who brought these up? I was left all alone, but these – where have they come from?"'

Isaiah prophesies that the land will become *'too small'* for its inhabitants – they will say, *'give us more space to live in'.* He also states that *'those who laid you waste depart from you',* *'those who devoured you will be far away'.*

And Moses promised: *'God will put the fear and terror of you on the whole land, wherever you go.'.* By YHWH removing her enemies far away the exiled Israelites are now free to come home and to occupy the biblical boundaries promised long ago to Israel – lands left vacant by their former enemies.

Obadiah 1:17 But on Mount Zion will be deliverance; it will be holy, and Jacob will possess his inheritance. 18 Jacob will be a fire and Joseph a flame; Esau will be stubble, and they will set him on fire and destroy him. There will be no survivors from Esau.' YHWH has spoken. 19 People from the Negev will occupy the mountains of Esau, and people from the foothills will possess the land of the Philistines. They will occupy the fields of Ephraim and Samaria, and Benjamin will possess Gilead. 20 This company of Israelite exiles who are in Canaan will possess the land as far as Zarephath; the exiles from Jerusalem who are in Sepharad will possess the towns of the Negev. 21 Deliverers will go up on Mount Zion to govern the mountains of Esau. And the kingdom will be YHWH's.

Both the *'mountains of Esau'* (Edom, i.e. southern Jordan) and the *'land of the Philistines'* (i.e. Gaza) will be occupied and possessed by Israel. Zarephath is today called Sarafand, a town in southern Lebanon, halfway between Tyre and Sidon.

Isaiah 11:10 In that day the Root of Jesse will stand as a banner for the peoples; the nations will rally to him, and his resting-place will be glorious. 11 In that day YHWH will reach out his hand a second time to reclaim the surviving remnant of his people from Assyria, from Lower Egypt, from Upper Egypt, from Cush, from Elam (Iran), from Babylonia, from Hamath (Hama, in Syria) and from the islands of the Medi-terranean. 12 He will raise a banner for the nations and gather the exiles of Israel; he will assemble the scattered people of Judah from the four quarters of the earth.

13 Ephraim's jealousy will vanish, and Judah's enemies will be destroyed; Ephraim will not be jealous of Judah, nor Judah hostile towards Ephraim.

14 They will swoop down on the slopes of Philistia to the west; together they will plunder the people to the east. They will subdue Edom and Moab, and the Ammonites will be subject to them.

15 YHWH will dry up the gulf of the Egyptian sea; with a scorching wind he will sweep his hand over the River Euphrates. He will break it up into seven streams so that anyone can cross over in sandals. 16 There will be a highway for the remnant of his people that is left from Assyria, as there was for Israel when they came up from Egypt.

Psalm 60:7-9 (also in **Psalm 108:9**) Gilead is mine, and Manasseh is mine; Ephraim is my helmet, Judah is my scepter.

8 <u>Moab</u> is my washbasin, on <u>Edom</u> I toss my sandal; over <u>Philistia</u> I shout in triumph." 9 Who will bring me to the fortified city? Who will lead me to Edom?

The Ingathering – summary:

1.   Israel will live in safety and *'no longer ... have malicious neighbours who are painful briers and sharp thorns'* (**Ezekiel 28:24-26, 34:22-31; Isaiah 19:16.17**)

2.   Israel will expand her territory and will control the resources of the Middle East. (**Isaiah 49:19,20; Deuteronomy 1:7,8, 11:24, Genesis 15:18**)

3.   The *'gulf of the Egyptian sea'* and the River Euphrates will be dried up. (**Isaiah 11:15**) The highway (from Egypt and Assyria) will be open for the ten tribes to return – the Ingathering! (**Isaiah 11:15,16, 19:23**)

4.   Iran will be scattered in exile around the world and will no longer be a nation (**Jeremiah 49:34-39**), Egypt will be in terror of Israel and subservient to her. (**Isaiah 9:16,17**) The modern-day nations of Syria, Lebanon and Jordan will probably no longer exist, (see 1, above), their population having abandoned their cities in *'fear and terror'* of Israel – and their lands becoming part of a *'greater Israel'*. (**Zechariah 12:6; Isaiah 17:9, 49:19,20**)

6 – Meet the Neighbours: Moab and Ammon

Psalm 83 lists the surrounding nations who will come against Israel in this attack. Asaph wrote down this prophecy long before the modern nations who inhabit the area came into existence, so he used the names for these people groups that were familiar to him at the time. This means we have to do a little research to identify those nations today. Here is the list:

> **Psalm 83:5** With one mind they plot together; they form an alliance against you – 6 the tents of Edom and the Ishmaelites, of Moab and the Hagrites, 7 Byblos, Ammon and Amalek, Philistia, with the people of Tyre. 8 Even Assyria has joined them to reinforce Lot's descendants.

Let us re-group those in Psalm 83 to simplify identification:

1. Moab and Ammon (Lot's descendants)
2. the Ishmaelites
3. the Hagrites
4. Byblos, the people of Tyre
5. Philistia
6. the tents of Edom
7. Amalek
8. Assyria

Moab and Ammon

Moab and Ammon were the sons of Abraham's nephew, Lot – the products of incest. Abraham gave Lot a choice of what land he wanted (of all that had been promised to Abraham) and Lot chose the Jordan Valley (at that time a very fertile place – before the destruction of Sodom and Gomorrah).

When Lot and his daughters fled from Sodom they lived in the mountains and the daughters made Lot drunk and in turn they slept with their father, both becoming pregnant as a result and producing two sons, Moab and Lo-ammi.

From these two men came the nations of Moab and Ammon, who occupied the area to the east of the river Jordan, Ammon to the north and Moab south of Ammon – corresponding to the north-east and centre of the modern-day Kingdom of Jordan. The capital of Jordan today is the city of Amman (i.e. Ammon).

We are given a brief history of the Moabites and Ammonites just before Israel crossed the Jordan to enter the promised land – between them they occupied the land which originally had belonged to a people called the Rephaites (also known to the Ammonites as Zamzummites and to the Moabites as Emites):

> **Deuteronomy 2:9** Then YHWH said to me, 'Do not harass the Moabites or provoke them to war, for I will not give you any part of their land. I have given Ar to the descendants of Lot as a possession.' 10 (<u>The Emites used to live there</u> – a people strong and numerous, and as tall as the Anakites. 11 Like the Anakites, they too were considered Rephaites, but the Moabites called them Emites.

> **Deuteronomy 2:20** (That too was considered a land of the Rephaites, who used to live there; but the Ammonites called them Zamzummites. 21 They were a people strong and numerous, and as tall as the Anakites. YHWH destroyed them from before <u>the Ammonites, who drove them out and settled in their place</u>.

Today we no longer hear of the individual nations of Moab and Ammon – their lands have become part of the Arab nation of Jordan. This was the fulfilment of a prophecy in Ezekiel, where their land would be taken over by the *'people from the east as a possession'*, i.e. by the Arabs, and that they *"will not be remembered among the nations"*:

Ezekiel 25 <u>A prophecy against Ammon</u>

> 1 The word of YHWH came to me: 2 'Son of man, <u>set your face against the Ammonites</u> and prophesy against them. 3 Say to them, "Hear the word of the Sovereign YHWH. This is what the Sovereign YHWH says: because you said 'Aha!' over my sanctuary when it was desecrated and over the land of Israel when it was laid waste and over the people of Judah when they went into exile, 4 therefore <u>I am going to give you to the people of the East as a possession</u>. They will set up their camps and pitch their tents among you; they will eat your fruit

and drink your milk. 5 I will turn Rabbah into a pasture for camels and Ammon [Amman] into a resting place for sheep. Then you will know that I am YHWH. 6 For this is what the Sovereign YHWH says: because you have clapped your hands and stamped your feet, rejoicing with all the malice of your heart against the land of Israel, 7 therefore I will stretch out my hand against you and give you as plunder to the nations. I will wipe you out from among the nations and exterminate you from the countries. I will destroy you, and you will know that I am YHWH.'"

A prophecy against Moab

8 'This is what the Sovereign YHWH says: "Because Moab and Seir said, 'Look, Judah has become like all the other nations,' 9 therefore I will expose the flank of Moab, beginning at its frontier towns – Beth Jeshimoth, Baal Meon and Kiriathaim – the glory of that land. 10 I will give Moab along with the Ammonites to the people of the East as a possession, so that the Ammonites will not be remembered among the nations; 11 and I will inflict punishment on Moab. Then they will know that I am YHWH.'"

So today Moab and Ammon no longer have separate identities – they are *'not remembered among the nations'* . Moab and Ammon still exist, but they have been absorbed into the Arab (Hashemite) Kingdom of Jordan. The future outlook for the nation of Jordan is not good:

Zephaniah 2:8 "I have heard the insults of Moab and the taunts of the Ammonites, who insulted my people and made threats against their land. 9 Therefore, as surely as I live," declares YHWH Almighty, the God of Israel, "surely Moab will become like Sodom, the Ammonites like Gomorrah—a place of weeds and salt pits, a wasteland forever. The remnant of my people will plunder them; the survivors of my nation will inherit their land." 10 This is what they will get in return for their pride, for insulting and mocking the people of YHWH Almighty. 11 YHWH will be awesome to them when he destroys all the gods of the earth. Distant nations will bow down to him, all of them in their own lands.

The land of modern-day Jordan (former Moab and Ammon) will be destroyed and plundered and will become the possession of Israel – a change from the case in Deuteronomy, where YHWH said he would NOT give them *'any part of their land'!* Now he says, *'the survivors of my nation* [i.e. Israel] *will inherit their land'* because of how they have threatened Israel.

Jeremiah gives another prophecy against Moab:

Jeremiah 48:2 Moab will be praised no more; in Heshbon people will plot her downfall: 'Come, let us put an end to that nation.' You, the people of Madmen, will also be silenced; the sword will pursue you. 3 Cries of anguish arise from Horonaim, cries of great havoc and destruction. 4 Moab will be broken; her little ones will cry out. 5 They go up the hill to Luhith, weeping bitterly as they go; on the road down to Horonaim anguished cries over the destruction are heard. 6 Flee! Run for your lives; become like a bush in the desert. 7 Since you trust in your deeds and riches, you too will be taken captive, and Chemosh [the Moabite god] will go into exile, together with his priests and officials. 8 The destroyer will come against every town, and not a town will escape. The valley will be ruined and the plateau destroyed, because YHWH has spoken. 9 Put salt on Moab, for she will be laid waste; her towns will become desolate, with no one to live in them.

15 Moab will be destroyed and her towns invaded; her finest young men will go down in the slaughter," declares the King, whose name is YHWH Almighty. 16 "The fall of Moab is at hand; her calamity will come quickly.

19 Stand by the road and watch, you who live in Aroer. Ask the man fleeing and the woman escaping, ask them, 'What has happened?' 20 Moab is disgraced, for she is shattered. Wail and cry out! Announce by the Arnon that Moab is destroyed.

28 Abandon your towns and dwell among the rocks, you who live in Moab. Be like a dove that makes its nest at the mouth of a cave.

42 Moab will be destroyed as a nation because she defied YHWH.

46 Woe to you, Moab! The people of Chemosh are destroyed; your sons are taken into exile and your daughters into captivity.

To summarise: Moab will no longer be a nation, her people will be *'taken captive, and will go into exile.' 'She will be laid waste, her towns will become desolate, with no-one to live in them.' 'Ask the man fleeing and the woman escaping.' 'Abandon your towns.' 'Moab will be destroyed as a nation because she defied YHWH.'*

Jeremiah 49:2 But the days are coming," declares YHWH, "when I will sound the battle cry against Rabbah [Amman] of the Ammonites; <u>it will become a mound of ruins</u>, and its surrounding villages will be set on fire. Then <u>Israel will drive out those who drove her out</u>," says YHWH.

5 <u>I will bring terror on you</u> from all those around you," declares YHWH, YHWH Almighty. "<u>Every one of you will be driven away, and no one will gather the fugitives</u>.

Jeremiah continues in the next chapter with a similar prophecy concerning Ammon – Rabbah *'will become a mound of ruins ... Israel will drive out those who drove her out ... every one of you will be driven away.'* The western part of northern Jordan (i.e. east of the Jordan river) was originally a part of Israel – the land of Gilead, where the tribes of Reuben and Gad originally settled. Ammon lived to the east of Reuben and Gad – i.e. north east Jordan today.

First, Moab and Ammon were to be taken over by *'the people from the east'* – i.e. the Arabs/Ishmaelites. This prophecy was fulfilled when Jordan became an Arab nation.

The second part of these prophecies will be fulfilled when Israel will invade and destroy Jordan. Although YHWH initially told Israel (back in Deuteronomy 2:9,20) that he would <u>not</u> give them the lands of Moab and Ammon – because of their hatred towards Israel over the centuries – He then promised that Israel would invade them and that they would flee into exile (as refugees), abandoning their towns to *'become desolate, with no-one to live in them'* – eventually being reclaimed by Israel.

Neighbours: Moab and Ammon

1. Nephews/grand-nephews of Abraham, through Lot's incest with his two daughters.

2. They took over the territory of the Rephaites – to the east of Israel (north-east and central Jordan, today).

3. When they arrived in the promised land, Israel were told by Moses that YHWH would not give them the lands of Moab and Ammon – but later, because of their hatred towards Israel, he promised Israel would take their land.

4. Ezekiel prophesied that Moab and Ammon would be *'given to the people of the east* [Arabs/Ishmaelites] *as a possession'* and would no longer have a separate identity – they *'will not be remembered among the nations.'* They are now known as the *Hashemite* (Arab) *Kingdom of Jordan*.

5. In future – according to Zephaniah and Jeremiah – Moab and Ammon (Jordan) will be invaded, become desolate, the people will be terrified and flee – driven away by Israel – and *'the survivors of [Israel] will inherit their land.'*

6. Amman, the capital of Jordan today, *'Rabbah of the Ammonites … will become a mound of ruins.'*

7 – Meet the Neighbours: The Ishmaelites

The Ishmaelites also are fairly easy to identify – Abraham was promised a son from whom a whole nation would come, but his wife, Sarah, was barren, so they decided to follow local custom at that time and have him sleep with Sarah's (Egyptian) maid, Hagar, as a surrogate mother. This plan backfired when the child, Ishmael, was born – because Hagar despised Sarah when she saw that she could conceive, but Sarah was unable to. (see Genesis 16)

Also, when the promised child, Isaac, was born, his older brother, Ishmael, was seen by Sarah mocking him. Sarah asked Abraham to send them both away, and Abraham did – after YHWH confirmed that Sarah was right to ask this. (see Genesis 21:1-20)

Genesis 21:20 Ishmael ... lived in the desert and became an archer. 21 While he was living in the Desert of Paran, his mother got a wife for him from Egypt.

Hagar had been given a prophecy about Ishmael:

Genesis 16:10 The angel added, 'I will increase your descendants so much that they will be too numerous to count.' 11 The angel of YHWH also said to her: You are now preg nant and you will give birth to a son. You shall name him Ishmael, for YHWH has heard of your misery. 12 He will be a wild donkey of a man; his hand will be against everyone and everyone's hand against him, and he will live in hostility towards all his brothers.'

Genesis 25:12 This is the account of the family line of Abraham's son Ishmael, whom Sarah's slave, Hagar the Egyptian, bore to Abraham. 13 These are the names of the sons of Ishmael, listed in the order of their birth: Nebaioth the first-born of Ishmael, Kedar, Adbeel, Mibsam, 14 Mishma, Dumah, Massa, 15 Hadad, Tema, Jetur, Naphish and Kedemah. 16 These were the sons of Ishmael, and these are the names of the twelve tribal rulers according to their settlements and camps.

17 Ishmael lived a hundred and thirty-seven years. He breathed his last and died, and he was gathered to his people. 18 His descendants settled in the area from Havilah to Shur, near the eastern border of Egypt, as you go towards Ashur. And they lived in hostility towards all the tribes related to them.

As the passage says, the sons of Ishmael gave their names to settlements and camps. Ezekiel lists people who traded with the kingdom of Tyre: "*Arabia and all the princes of Kedar were your customers; they did business with you in lambs, rams and goats.*" (Ezekiel 27:21) Kedar was Ishmael's second son, here linked with Arabia. Kedar is again associated with Arabia in Isaiah 21:13-17. The firstborn son of Ishmael, Nebaioth, gave his name to the Arab Nabataeans – the people who built the rock city of Petra.

Isaiah seems to predict that Saudi Arabia will bring their wealth to Israel:

Isaiah 60:4 'Lift up your eyes and look about you: all assemble and come to you; your sons come from afar, and your daughters are carried on the hip. 5 Then you will look and be radiant, your heart will throb and swell with joy; the wealth on the seas will be brought to you, to you the riches of the nations will come. 6 Herds of camels will cover your land, young camels of Midian and Ephah. And all from Sheba will come, bearing gold and incense and proclaiming the praise of YHWH. 7 All Kedar's flocks will be gathered to you, the rams of Nebaioth will serve you; they will be accepted as offerings on my altar, and I will adorn my glorious temple.

Midian is north-eastern Saudi Arabia. The kingdom of Saba, and the Sabeans were located in the south of Arabia. Kedar and Nebaioth were sons of Ishmael. So the modern embodiment of the Ishmaelites are the Arab nations and, in particular, today's Kingdom of Saudi Arabia.

Ishmaelites – summary:

1. Abraham's first-born son, through his wife's maid, Hagar – mocked his younger brother, Isaac, through whom the promises were to be fulfilled.

2. Prophesied to become *'a wild donkey of a man … he will live in hostility towards all his brothers.'* *'They lived in hostility towards all the tribes related to them.'*

3. Ismael was father to twelve sons: Nebaioth – the Nabateans, who built the rock city of Petra; Kedar – *'the princes of Kedar';* and ten more tribal rulers – known to us collectively as the Arabs of Arabia.

4. Isaiah prophesied that the riches of Arabia – Nebaioth, Kedar, Midian, etc. – would be brought to adorn the temple in Jerusalem.

5. The Ishmaelites can be identified as the Arabs in general and of Saudi Arabia in particular.

8 – Meet the Neighbours: The Hagrites

The Hagrites (or Hagarenes) are a little bit less obvious – 1st Chronicles 5 mentions them when describing the area occupied by the Israelite tribe of Reuben:

> **1st Chronicles 5:8** They [Reuben] settled in the area from Aroer to Nebo and Baal Meon. 9 To the east they occupied the land up to the edge of the desert that extends to the River Euphrates, because their livestock had increased in Gilead.
>
> 10 During Saul's reign they waged war against the Hagrites, who were defeated at their hands; they occupied the dwellings of the Hagrites throughout the entire region east of Gilead.

Reuben lived in the land of Gilead, east of the Jordan river, and Gad and Manasseh in Bashan to the north of them, equivalent to the (Israeli held) Golan Heights today (one of the towns of Manasseh was actually called Golan – **Deuteronomy 4:43; Joshua 20:8; 21:27; 1 Chronicle 6:71**).

The tribe of Reuben occupied the Hagrite land *'east of Gilead'* – which would place the Hagrites in the Golan area of modern-day Syria and eastward towards the Euphrates river. Reuben were assisted in this conflict by their fellow tribes of Gad and Manasseh:

> **1st Chronicles 5:21** They [Reuben, Gad and Manasseh] seized the livestock of the Hagrites – fifty thousand camels, two hundred and fifty thousand sheep and two thousand donkeys. They also took one hundred thousand people captive, 22 and many others fell slain, because the battle was God's. And they occupied the land until the exile.

By taking so many people of the Hagrites as captives the three Israelite tribes allowed them to survive and occupy the area after the ten tribes were taken into captivity. So the Hagrites are today a part of modern Syria.

Isaiah refers specifically to Damascus, now the capital of Syria – although verses 12-14 extend this prophecy also to the *'peoples'* and *'many nations'*, who rage against, loot and plunder (Israel):

> **Isaiah 17:1** The oracle concerning Damascus. "Behold, <u>Damascus is about to be removed from being a city And will become a fallen ruin</u>. 2 "The cities of Aroer are forsaken; They will be for flocks to lie down in, And there will be no one to frighten them. 3 "The fortified city will disappear from Ephraim, <u>and sovereignty from Damascus and the remnant of Aram</u>; They will be like the glory of the sons of Israel," Declares YHWH of hosts.
>
> 9 In that day <u>their strong cities will be like forsaken places in the forest</u>, Or like branches which they abandoned <u>before the sons of Israel; And the land will be a desolation</u>.

Damascus will *'be removed from being a city and will become a fallen ruin'. 'Sovereignty* [will disappear] *from Damascus and the remnant of Aram.'* (Syria) *'Their strong cities will be like forsaken places ... which they abandoned before the sons of Israel.'* Syria will flee before Israel and their cities will be abandoned.

In Joshua, where the promised boundaries of Israel are defined, mention is made of Hamath, which is still a city today – Hama, in northern Syria.

> **Joshua 13** 1 When Joshua had grown old, YHWH said to him, "You are now very old, and there are still very large areas of land to be taken over. 2 "<u>This is the land that remains</u>: ...
>
> 4 all the land of the Canaanites, from Arah of the Sidonians as far as Aphek and the border of the Amorites; 5 the area of <u>Byblos; and all Lebanon to the east, from Baal Gad below Mount Hermon to Lebo Hamath</u>. 6 "As for all the inhabitants of the mountain regions from Lebanon to Misrephoth Maim, that is, all the Sidonians, <u>I myself will drive them out before the Israelites. Be sure to allocate this land to Israel for an inheritance</u>, as I have instructed you, 7 and divide it as an inherit-ance among the nine tribes and half of the tribe of Manasseh.

So Hama (Hamath) in Syria was always intended to be a part of Israel.

> **Jeremiah 49:23** <u>Concerning Damascus. "Hamath and Arpad are put to shame</u>, For they have heard bad news; They are disheartened. There is anxiety by the sea, It cannot be calmed.

24 "Damascus has become helpless; She has turned away to flee, And panic has gripped her; Distress and pangs have taken hold of her Like a woman in childbirth. 25 "How the city of praise has not been deserted, The town of My joy! 26 "Therefore, her young men will fall in her streets, And all the men of war will be silenced in that day," declares YHWH of hosts. 27 "I will set fire to the wall of Damascus, And it will devour the fortified towers of Ben-hadad."

'Damascus has become helpless, she has turned away to flee, and panic has gripped her.' Founded in the third millennium BCE, the old city of **Damascus** is considered to be among the oldest continually inhabited cities in the world.

Modern-day Syria, then, is easily identified, and will flee in panic before Israel. As Asaph says in Psalm 83, *'like tumble-weed before a gale.'*

The Hagrites – summary:

1. Originally lived in the desert east of Reuben, towards the Euphrates, i.e. in southern Syria today.

2. Joshua mentions Hamath (now Hama in Syria) as part of the territory allotted to Israel.

3. Isaiah 17 prophesies destruction against Damascus and other cities of Aram (Syria).

4. Jeremiah says, *'Damascus … has turned away to flee, and panic has gripped her'* – the fear of YHWH!

5. Syria will abandon their cities and flee before Israel into exile.

9 – Meet the Neighbours: Byblos and the people of Tyre

Byblos (Gebal in some translations) and the people of Tyre are also quite easy to identify, as these two former Phoenician cities – Byblos and Tyre (also called Sour) – are still inhabited cities of the modern-day nation of Lebanon.

Byblos was originally called Gebal, then re-named by the Greeks. Tyre, Sidon, Byblos and *'all Lebanon'* were originally intended to become part of the Israelite homeland:

> **Joshua 13** 1 When Joshua had grown old, YHWH said to him, "You are now very old, and there are still very large areas of land to be taken over. 2 "This is the land that remains: all the regions of the Philistines ... 4 on the south; all the land of the Canaanites, from Arah of the **Sidonians** as far as Aphek and the border of the Amorites; 5 the area of **Byblos**; and all **Lebanon** to the east, from Baal Gad below Mount Hermon to Lebo **Hamath**. 6 "As for all the inhabitants of the mountain regions from **Lebanon** to Misrephoth Maim, that is, all the **Sidonians**, I myself will drive them out before the Israelites. Be sure to allocate this land to Israel for an inheritance, as I have instructed you, 7 and divide it as an inheritance among the nine tribes and half of the tribe of Manasseh."

As we said in the last chapter, Hamath is today called Hama, in Syria, north of the Lebanese border – so all of modern-day Lebanon was meant to be included in the *'promised land'*. YHWH said to Joshua that he himself would *'drive the Sidonians out before the Israelites. Be sure to allocate this land to Israel for an inheritance.'*

> **Joel 3:4** 'Now what have you against me, Tyre and Sidon and all you regions of Philistia? Are you repaying me for something I have done? If you are paying me back, I will swiftly and speedily return on your own heads what you have done. 5 For you took my silver and my gold and carried off my finest treasures to your temples. 6 You sold the people of Judah and

Jerusalem to the Greeks, that you might send them far from their homeland.

7 'See, I am going to rouse them out of the places to which you sold them, and I will return on your own heads what you have done. 8 I will sell your sons and daughters to the people of Judah, and they will sell them to the Sabeans, a nation far away.' YHWH has spoken.

Here is motivation – *'You* [Tyre, Sidon and Philistia] *sold the people of Judah and Jerusalem to the Greeks, that you might send them far from their homeland.'*

Deuteronomy 1:6 the land of the Canaanites and to Lebanon, as far as the great river, the Euphrates. 8 See, I have given you this land. Go in and take possession of the land that YHWH swore he would give to your fathers – to Abraham, Isaac and Jacob – and to their descendants after them.'

Right back in Moses' time God had planned for Lebanon to be an integral part of the promised land!

Lebanon was originally the only Christian state in the Middle East. It was designed as such from its creation by France – given the mandate over Syria by the League of Nations in 1920 – who then did a deal with the UK to take over part of the original territory promised to the Jewish state. This was in exchange for Britain having control of the oil-rich region around Kirkuk in Iraq – now part of the *Kurdish Autonomous Area*.

Beirut in the sixties was known as *'the Paris of the Middle East'* – a popular tourist destination until 1975. However, it did not remain a Christian state because more and more Muslim Arabs poured into Lebanon – partly as a result of the Israel War of Independence in 1948 and the Six Day War in 1967.

Muslims eventually became the majority in Lebanon, and began to take control, resulting in a Muslim/Christian civil war between the Maronite Christians who had until then ruled the country, and the PLO (Palestine Liberation Organisation) – which lasted from 1975 to 1990, taking around 120,000 lives.

Syria became involved in the conflict in 1976 and continued to occupy the country until 2005. In retaliation for ongoing rocket attacks against Galilee, Israel invaded south Lebanon in 1982 and when Israel eventually withdrew, in 2,000, the Iranian-backed Shi'ite militia – Hezbollah – began to grow in strength, until today they wield major power within Lebanon.

Their power-base in Lebanon has been enhanced by their battle experience of participation in the Syrian civil war, and they have hundreds of thousands of rockets currently aimed into Israel from southern Lebanon. A war erupted between Israel and Hezbollah in 2006 and an uneasy truce has continued since then.

> **Ezekiel 28** A prophecy against Sidon 20 The word of YHWH came to me: 21 'Son of man, set your face against Sidon; prophesy against her 22 and say: "This is what the Sovereign YHWH says: "'I am against you, Sidon, and among you I will display my glory. You will know that I am YHWH, when I inflict punishment on you and within you am proved to be holy. 23 I will send a plague upon you and make blood flow in your streets. The slain will fall within you, with the sword against you on every side. Then you will know that I am YHWH. 24 "'No longer will the people of Israel have malicious neighbours who are painful briers and sharp thorns. Then they will know that I am the Sovereign YHWH. 25 "'This is what the Sovereign YHWH says: when I gather the people of Israel from the nations where they have been scattered, I will be proved holy through them in the sight of the nations. Then they will live in their own land, which I gave to my servant Jacob. 26 They will live there in safety and will build houses and plant vineyards; they will live in safety when I inflict punishment on all their neighbours who maligned them. Then they will know that I am YHWH their God."'

Hezbollah are currently *'malicious neighbours'* to Israel, acting as *'painful briers and sharp thorns'*. Through Ezekiel God is promising to *'inflict punishment on'* these people and that Israel then *'will live there* [in Lebanon] *in safety and will build houses and plant vineyards.'*

Byblos and Tyre – summary:

1. Both Byblos and Tyre are still in existence as cities in Lebanon today.

2. *'All Lebanon'* and beyond was designated as part of the land promised to Israel by YHWH in Joshua 13.

3. Lebanon is now a Muslim-majority Arab state, partly controlled by the Shi'ite Hezbollah militia, who have gained battle experience in Syria and – with the support of Iran – have amassed thousands of rockets, which are now aimed at Israel.

4. God has promised to *'inflict punishment on'* Lebanon (and all Israel's neighbours).

5. Israel *'will live there* (in Lebanon) *in safety and build houses and plant vineyards.'*

10 – Meet the Neighbours: Philistia

Philistia was the kingdom of the Philistine people – originally of Greek (Cretan) origin and eventually completely wiped out by Israel – as prophesied in Amos and Zephaniah. The five cities of Gaza, Ashkelon, Ashdod, Ekron and Gath were city-states of the ancient Philistines. All but Gaza are today re-built modern cities within Israel.

Gaza is the main city of the Palestinian-controlled area of the Gaza Strip – ruled by the terror organisation, Hamas (meaning *'resistance'* in Arabic). Control of the area was given to the Palestinian Authority by Israel in 2005. After the 2006 Palestinian election Hamas promptly took over the entire Strip, murdering many of the opposition Fatah supporters in the process. There have been continual terror attacks incited by Hamas against Israel since, escalating into three major conflicts – in 2006, 2008 and 2014.

The land of the Philistines (Gaza) was specifically included in the original promised land:

Joshua 13:1-3 When Joshua had grown old, YHWH said to him, 'You are now very old, and there are still very large areas of land to be taken over.

2 'This is the land that remains: all the regions of the Philistines and Geshurites, 3 from the River Shihor on the east of Egypt to the territory of Ekron on the north, all of it counted as Canaanite though held by the five Philistine rulers in Gaza, Ashdod, Ashkelon, Gath and Ekron; the territory of the Avvites.

The Philistines originated from Crete (Caphtor). They invaded from the sea and took over the land formerly occupied by the Avvites:

Deuteronomy 2:23 And as for the Avvites who lived in villages as far as Gaza, the Caphtorites coming out from Caphtor destroyed them and settled in their place.

Jeremiah 47:4 YHWH is about to destroy the Philistines, the remnant from the coasts of Caphtor (Crete).

Amos 9:7 'Are not you Israelites the same to me as the Cushites?' declares YHWH. 'Did I not bring Israel up from Egypt, the Philistines from Caphtor and the Arameans from Kir?

A recent archaeological excavation (July 2019) near Gath – led by the well-known Professor Yossef Garfinkel – has uncovered an ancient Philistine settlement, thought to be the biblical Ziglag, where David hid from Saul. DNA tests on Philistine bones found there show they came from southern Europe – confirming what was stated in Deuteronomy, Jeremiah and Amos.

Amos 1:6 This is what YHWH says: 'For three sins of Gaza, even for four, I will not relent. Because she took captive whole communities and sold them to Edom, 7 I will send fire on the walls of Gaza that will consume her fortresses. 8 I will destroy the king of Ashdod and the one who holds the sceptre in Ashkelon. I will turn my hand against Ekron, till the last of the Philistines are dead,' says the Sovereign YHWH.

Zephaniah 2:4 Gaza will be abandoned and Ashkelon left in ruins. At midday Ashdod will be emptied and Ekron uprooted. 5 Woe to you who live by the sea, you Kerethite people; the word of YHWH is against you, Canaan, land of the Philistines. He says, 'I will destroy you, and none will be left.' 6 The land by the sea will become pastures having wells for shepherds and sheepfolds for flocks. 7 That land will belong to the remnant of the people of Judah; there they will find pasture. In the evening they will lie down in the houses of Ashkelon. YHWH their God will care for them; he will restore their fortunes.

Ezekiel 25 A prophecy against Philistia

15 'This is what the Sovereign YHWH says: "Because the Philistines acted in vengeance and took revenge with malice in their hearts, and with ancient hostility sought to destroy Judah, 16 therefore this is what the Sovereign YHWH says: I am about to stretch out my hand against the Philistines, and I will wipe out the Kerethites and destroy those remaining along the coast. 17 I will carry out great vengeance on them and punish them in my wrath. Then they will know that I am YHWH, when I take vengeance on them."'

Obadiah 1:19 people from the foothills will possess the land of the Philistines. 20 This company of Israelite exiles who are in

<u>Canaan will possess the land</u> 21 ... And <u>the kingdom will be YHWH's</u>.

YHWH says, *'I will turn my hand against Ekron, till the last of the Philistines are dead!'* (Amos); *"I will destroy you, and none will be left.' (Zephaniah) and, 'I will wipe out the Kerethites [Philistines] and destroy those remaining along the coast,'* (Ezekiel).

The ancient Philistines were destroyed by Israel and disappeared from history around 1,000 BCE. Israel have re-built four of their five cities, but the Gaza Strip is now occupied by Palestinian Arabs, led by Hamas, having been handed back to the Palestinian Authority by Ariel Sharon in 2005.

The Hamas control Gaza and want to destroy Israel – they state: *"Israel will exist and will continue to exist until Islam will obliterate it, just as it obliterated others before it."* Hamas Charter – para 2*

There are no longer any Philistines living in Gaza, or anywhere else – so these prophesies have been partly fulfilled, but Zephaniah also says that *'their land* – including Gaza – *will belong to the people of Judah'* and *'Israelite exiles ... will possess the land.'* This part of the prophecies has yet to be fulfilled.

Although the 'Palestinian' people who live there today are mainly descended from the Edomites – mixed with various Arab nations (see next chapter) – we can identify Philistia today as the area of the Hamas-controlled Gaza Strip.

Incidentally, Psalm 83 seems to link together Gaza and Tyre – i.e. Hamas and Hezbollah – verse 7 states, *'Philistia, <u>with</u> the people of Tyre',* implying a linkage between them – *'with'*.

Philistia – summary:

1. Originally from Crete, the Philistines were intransigent enemies of Israel, who disappeared from history around

---

*avalon.law.yale.edu/20th_century/hamas.asp

1,000 BCE – as prophesied by Amos – *'till the last of the Philistines are dead';* and Zephaniah – *'none will be left.'*

2. DNA tests on Philistine bones confirm they originated in southern Europe.

3. Joshua declared that all of the Philistine cities were to become part of Israel. (Joshua 13:3) Four of the five cities of the Philistines are now re-built as modern cities in Israel – only Gaza remains, having been handed back to the 'Palestinians' by Ariel Sharon in 2005.

4. The inhabitants of Gaza today still exhibit that *'ancient hostility'* attributed to the Philistines.

5. Ultimately, *'Gaza ... will belong to the remnant of the people of Judah.'* (Zephaniah 2:4,7)

11 – Meet the Neighbours: The tents of Edom

'The tents of Edom' is an interesting phrase, suggesting a people of impermanence, transient – refugees even? Edom (meaning red) comes from Esau, brother of Jacob (Israel) and he developed a great hatred for his brother – though they were reconciled for a time.

> **Genesis 27:41** Esau held a grudge against Jacob because of the blessing his father had given him. He said to himself, 'The days of mourning for my father are near; then I will kill my brother Jacob.'

That enmity between Edom and the nation of Israel continued down through the centuries. Like the aforementioned Moab and Ammon, Edom no longer exists as a separate nation. So what became of this people and can we identify them today?

> **Deuteronomy 2:12** Horites used to live in Seir, but the descendants of Esau drove them out. They destroyed the Horites from before them and settled in their place, just as Israel did in the land YHWH gave them as their possession.

> **Deuteronomy 2:22** YHWH had done the same for the descendants of Esau, who lived in Seir, when he destroyed the Horites from before them. They drove them out and have lived in their place to this day.

Edom/Esau took over land that once was home to the Horites. Their land was originally to the south of modern-day Jordan – including Petra, though the ancient capital of Edom was Bozrah, further north – stretching south into part of what is now Saudi Arabia: Mount Seir, Teman and Dedan.

Moses was told by YHWH (**Numbers 20:14-21**) that the Israelites were to avoid war with their brothers and so they detoured around the territory of Edom to the west. King David later conquered Edom and the nation became subject to Israel for some time after.

Later in time they began to be pushed from the east by the Nabataeans – Arab descendants of Nebaioth, eldest son of Ishmael – and when Nebuchadnezzar, king of Babylon, conquered the Kingdom of Judah and took the Jews captive to Babylon, the Edomites took advantage of Judah's destruction to move west and north into the land of southern Israel and occupy it.

They were around in the time of Ezra and Nehemiah and – along with Philistines, Ammonites and Arabs – hindered the returning Jews in their re-building of the Temple and City of Jerusalem. This area (of southern Israel) later became known by the Greek name, *Idumea*, and the city of Hebron became their capital.

During the time of the Maccabees the Idumaeans were conquered by Judas Maccabeus and later by John Hyrcanus, who forced them to convert to Judaism in 110 BCE:

> 'Hyrcanus took also Dora and Marissa, cities of Idumea, and subdued all the Idumeans; and permitted them to stay in that country, if they would circumcise their genitals, and make use of the laws of the Jews; and they were so desirous of living in the country of their forefathers, that they submitted to the use of circumcision, and of the rest of the Jewish ways of living; at which time therefore this befell them, that they were hereafter no other than Jews.'
>
> (Josephus, Antiquities of the Jews, XIII, Chapter 9)

Antipater, the father of Herod the Great, was of Edomite/ Idumaean ancestry and the Idumaeans were still around in New Testament times:

> **Mark 3:7-9** Jesus withdrew with his disciples to the lake, and a large crowd from Galilee followed. 8 When they heard all he was doing, many people came to him from Judea, Jerusalem, Idumaea, and the regions across the Jordan and around Tyre and Sidon.

When Roman general, Titus, destroyed Jerusalem in 70 AD the Zealots were aided by 20,000 Idumaeans, who were besieged in the temple. The Romans attacked Idumaea also and many Idumaeans were killed or sent away into slavery – however, the Romans spared 40,000 of them, fulfilling the prophecies of Obadiah and Jeremiah, that they would become *'small among the nations'*:

Chapter 11 – Meet the Neighbours: The tents of Edom

Obadiah 1:1 The vision of Obadiah. This is what the Sovereign YHWH says about Edom—

We have heard a message from YHWH: An envoy was sent to the nations to say, "Rise, let us go against her for battle"— 2 "See, I will make you small among the nations; you will be utterly despised. 3 The pride of your heart has deceived you, you who live in the clefts of the rocks and make your home on the heights, you who say to yourself, 'Who can bring me down to the ground?' 4 Though you soar like the eagle and make your nest among the stars, from there I will bring you down," declares YHWH. 5 "If thieves came to you, if robbers in the night—oh, what a disaster awaits you!—would they not steal only as much as they wanted? If grape pickers came to you, would they not leave a few grapes? 6 But how Esau will be ransacked, his hidden treasures pillaged! 7 All your allies will force you to the border; your friends will deceive and overpower you; those who eat your bread will set a trap for you, but you will not detect it.

8 "In that day," declares YHWH, "will I not destroy the wise men of Edom, those of understanding in the mountains of Esau? 9 Your warriors, Teman, will be terrified, and everyone in Esau's mountains will be cut down in the slaughter. 10 Because of the violence against your brother Jacob, you will be covered with shame; you will be destroyed forever. 11 On the day you stood aloof while strangers carried off his wealth and foreigners entered his gates and cast lots for Jerusalem, you were like one of them. 12 You should not gloat over your brother in the day of his misfortune, nor rejoice over the people of Judah in the day of their destruction, nor boast so much in the day of their trouble. 13 You should not march through the gates of my people in the day of their disaster, nor gloat over them in their calamity in the day of their disaster, nor seize their wealth in the day of their disaster. 14 You should not wait at the crossroads to cut down their fugitives, nor hand over their survivors in the day of their trouble.

15 "The day of YHWH is near for all nations. As you have done, it will be done to you; your deeds will return upon your own head. 16 Just as you drank on my holy hill, so all the nations will drink continually; they will drink and drink and be as if they had never been.

17 But on Mount Zion will be deliverance; it will be holy, and Jacob will possess his inheritance. 18 Jacob will be a fire and Joseph a flame; Esau will be stubble, and they will set him on fire and destroy him. There will be no survivors from Esau." YHWH has spoken.

19 <u>People from the Negev will occupy the mountains of Esau, and people from the foothills will possess the land of the Philistines.</u> They will occupy the fields of Ephraim and Samaria, and Benjamin will possess Gilead. 20 <u>This company of Israelite exiles who are in Canaan will possess the land</u> as far as Zarephath; the exiles from Jerusalem who are in Sepharad will possess the towns of the Negev. 21 Deliverers will go up on Mount Zion to govern the mountains of Esau. And the kingdom will be YHWH's.

Jeremiah 49:15 "<u>Now I will make you small among the nations, despised by mankind</u>. 16 The terror you inspire and the pride of your heart have deceived you, you who live in the clefts of the rocks, who occupy the heights of the hill. Though you build your nest as high as the eagle's, from there I will bring you down," declares YHWH. 17 "<u>Edom will become an object of horror; all who pass by will be appalled and will scoff because of all its wounds</u>. 18 As Sodom and Gomorrah were overthrown, along with their neighbouring towns," says YHWH, "so no one will live there; no people will dwell in it. 19 "Like a lion coming up from Jordan's thickets to a rich pastureland, <u>I will chase Edom from its land in an instant</u>.

Let's concentrate on the main points from Obadiah's and Jeremiah's prophecies:

Obadiah 1:2 "<u>See, I will make you small among the nations; you will be utterly despised</u>.

7 <u>All your allies will force you to the border</u>; your friends will deceive and overpower you; those who eat your bread will set a trap for you, but you will not detect it.

10 <u>Because of the violence</u> (Heb: hamas) <u>against your brother Jacob, you will be covered with shame; you will be destroyed forever</u>.

15 <u>As you have done, it will be done to you; your deeds will return upon your own head</u>.

Jeremiah 49:15 "<u>Now I will make you small among the nations, despised by mankind</u>.

The Edomites/'Palestinians' have certainly become a people who are despised by the world – and especially by their Arab brothers. They have been *'forced to the border'* by their fellow Arabs. Ezekiel and Malachi also have something to say about Edom:

Ezekiel 25 <u>A prophecy against Edom</u>

12 'This is what the Sovereign YHWH says: "<u>Because Edom took revenge on Judah</u> and became very guilty by doing so, 13 therefore this is what the Sovereign YHWH says: <u>I will stretch out my hand against Edom and kill both man and beast. I will lay it waste,</u> and from Teman to Dedan they will fall by the sword. 14 I will take vengeance on Edom <u>by the hand of my people Israel</u>, and they will deal with Edom in accordance with my anger and my wrath; they will know my vengeance, declares the Sovereign YHWH.'"

Malachi 1:2 'Was not Esau Jacob's brother?' declares YHWH. 'Yet I have loved Jacob, 3 but <u>Esau I have hated, and I have turned his hill country into a wasteland</u> and left his inheritance to the desert jackals.'

4 Edom may say, 'Though we have been crushed, we will re-build the ruins.' But this is what YHWH Almighty says: 'They may build, but I will demolish. <u>They will be called the Wicked Land, a people always under the wrath of YHWH</u>. 5 You will see it with your own eyes and say, "Great is YHWH – even beyond the borders of Israel!"'

The Edomites/Idumeans/Palestinians are scattered today in various parts of the Middle East and around the world. They have attempted to build – i.e. a 'Palestinian' State in the 'West Bank' and Gaza Strip – but YHWH says, *'I will demolish.'* The Palestinian Authority set up under the *Oslo Accords* has been a disaster – non-democratic, corrupt, division and conflict between Hamas and Fatah, spending the billions they receive in aid on terror, instead of the good of their people.

While the fledgling State of Israel were able, within a few years, to absorb around 850,000 refugees from the Arab states of the Middle East and North Africa – those same Arab states, many of them rich from oil exports (Saudia Arabia, Libya and the Gulf States), were unwilling to absorb the 550,000 displaced Palestinians – instead they were used as pawns to foment hatred against Israel and to keep the wound festering right up to the present day.

The majority of those remaining in the Middle East still live in refugee camps. The Kingdom of Jordan has a population of 10 million, of which over 2 million are registered Palestinian refugees, living in ten refugee camps. The Gaza Strip, though administered autonomously by Hamas since Israel moved out in 2005, still has eight refugee camps, containing 1.4 million refugees. In Judaea and Samaria (the so-called 'West Bank'), under the autonomous rule of the *Palestinian Authority,* there are nineteen camps, containing 809,700 registered refugees.

In Lebanon there are twelve Palestinian refugee camps, with almost 458,000 registered refugees; and in war-torn Syria there are thirteen camps, with almost 552,000 registered refugees. That is a total of sixty-two refugee camps, and more than 5 million people – from an original 550,000! – who are dependent entirely upon UNWRA (Relief and Works Agency) for their daily provision.

This does not include the 1.9 million Palestinians living securely in Israel and another 2.25 million who have managed to emigrate to other countries – such as the USA, Chile, Saudi Arabia, etc. Around 240,000 Palestinians live in Saudi Arabia. They are not allowed to apply for Saudi citizenship because of Arab League instructions barring Arab states from granting them citizenship.

On my first ever visit to Israel I walked the short distance from the centre of Jerusalem to the Old City's Jaffa Gate and witnessed an UNWRA truck handing out bags of flour to Arab men with hand trucks, who were then wheeling it away to their homes.

All other refugees around the world come under the UNHCR (High Commission for Refugees) and – apart from more recent wars and disasters – have largely been settled and housed. Only UNRWA perpetuates the refugee situation, so that more and more *'refugees'* are added, to the third, fourth and fifth generations. This is only building up and sustaining the *'everlasting hatred'* that already exists.

I think that if I were a Palestinian refugee – living in a crowded and sub-standard camp, with little hope of life ever changing or improving – and being told every day that the Jews and Israel were entirely responsible for my situation – then I might be angry at Israel, too! But this despicable treatment comes not from Israel, but from their fellow-Arabs. Israel took care of their incoming Jewish refugees – but the Arabs and Islam have only cynically used these people to further their political aims.

In 135 AD the Romans re-named the whole area – deliberately using the extinct name of Israel's hated enemies, the Philistines, calling it *Syria Palaestina*. So the Idumeans who remained there became citizens of *Syria Palestina* i.e. they became Palestinians. This name – *Palestine* – unfortunately, was reinstated by Britain when they took over the League of Nations Mandate in 1920.

Down the centuries, while most Jews were forced to flee the land, the Idumeans – who were never truly Jews, but forced converts – remained on the land by converting when forced to the religion of their conquerors – be that Islam, Christianity (during Crusader rule), or Islam once again. In the process there were probably some real Jews included as there are some Arab villages in the area today where the elders will admit in private to having Jewish ancestry*.

When the area was given (temporarily, I might add) into the hands of Britain, with a Mandate to develop a Jewish National Home – under the auspices of the *League of Nations* and the *San Remo Agreement* of 1922, which adopted the *Balfour Declaration* of 1917 – the British firstly copied the Roman insult by renaming the area *Palestine* (it had been the province of *Southern Syria* under the Turks), then began carving pieces off the original territory. First, they gave the area south of the Litani River to the new state of Lebanon and the Golan Heights to Syria (concessions to France, who held the Mandate for these two areas).

Then, in 1922, the British handed over more than three quarters (78%) of what remained – creating the new state of Trans-Jordan. Britain – due to anti-Semitism – totally reneged on their duty to fulfil the mandate they had been given.

The newly formed *United Nations* then decided to divide even this small remnant into two separate states – one for Jews, one for Arabs. What eventually became Israel was only a very small part (< 20%) of the area originally designated for the Jewish Homeland.

The only people to ever call themselves *Palestinians* up to that point were the Jewish residents – though when Israel became a state in 1948 they naturally dropped the *Palestinian* label and became Israelis! The Arab population rejected the title, *Palestinians,* preferring to simply be called Arabs.

---

* Tsvi Misinai – *Brother Shall Not Lift His Sword Against Brother:* The Roots and Solution to the Problem in the Holy Land

Although Jordan had illegally annexed the *'West Bank'* in 1948 (recognised only by Britain and Pakistan) and it was under their (Arab) rule for nineteen years, none of the inhabitants showed any desire to create a separate state. Arab *Palestinians* only came into existence in 1964, when Egyptian Yasser Arafat created the terrorist PLO (Palestine Liberation Organisation).

Many of those now claiming to be *'Palestinians'* were Arab immigrants from the surrounding countries, who moved to Palestine between 1832 and 1947 because of the improved prosperity brought to the land by the incoming Jews. Under the British mandate roads and power stations were built – a whole new infrastructure.

The Jews provided work in their newly planted citrus orchards and vineyards, as well as in factories and construction. From the 1920s until the end of the British Mandate (in 1948) Arab populations increased dramatically in areas close to Jewish settlement, but actually dwindled in those areas – such as Hebron and Gaza – where there was no Jewish settlement.[*]

In 2012 a former Hamas Minister of the Interior, Gaza-based Fathi Hammad, said in an interview with *Al Hikmat TV*:

> "We all have Arab roots. Every Palestinian in Gaza and throughout Palestine can prove his Arab roots, whether from Saudi Arabia, Yemen, or anywhere ... Half of my family is Egyptian ... More than 30 clans in the Gaza Strip are called Al-Masri (the Egyptian). Half of the Palestinians are Egyptians."

No, the future for the people of Edom – the Edomites, who became *Idumeans*, then finally *'Palestinians'* – does not look good! According to the Hebrew prophets, Edom will be destroyed by Israel and their land will become *'a wasteland'* – taken over by Israel.

By the sound of these prophecies, the existing five million Palestinian refugees will only be a drop in a bucket compared to the overall Arab/Iranian refugee situation created by the *Six Hour War* – of their own making, once again. We may be talking of a total of one hundred million – dead, or displaced!

---

*The Claim of Dispossession – Arieh L. Avneri

The tents of Edom – summary:

1. The phrase *'the tents of Edom'* suggests impermanence – refugees, even?

2. Edom was Esau, brother of Jacob, who became known as Israel.

3. Esau *'held a grudge against Jacob'* and decided he would *'kill* [his] *brother Jacob.'* That *'ancient hostility'* is being continued today.

4. When Babylon conquered Judah and took the Jews captive, the Edomites took advantage and moved west and north into southern Israel. Hebron became their new capital. The Greeks called it *Idumaea*

5. The Idumaeans were forcibly converted to Judaism by Judaean ruler, John Hyrcanus in 110 BCE.

6. Obadiah and Jeremiah said the Edomites would become, *'small among the nations, despised.'* This happened when the Romans almost wiped them out in 135 CE, leaving only 40,000 survivors.

7. The Romans re-named the area *Syria Palaestina* and the British deliberately revived this insulting name, *Palestine*, when they took over the Mandate in 1920.

8. Even so the only people calling themselves *'Palestinians'* were Jewish – up until the State of Israel came into being in 1948.

9. *Palestinian* – as a designation for Arabs – only came into existence in 1964, when the PLO terrorist organisation was set up by Egyptian, Yasser Arafat.

10. Of approximately nine million Palestinians around the world today, five million of them still live in refugee camps – in Gaza, West Bank, Jordan, Syria and Lebanon – mostly areas outside Israel's jurisdiction. The biblical *'tents of Edom'* seems a very appropriate designation.

12 – Meet the Neighbours: The Amalekites

Amalek was the grandson of Esau, through his son, Eliphaz, and so inherited the *'everlasting hatred'* from Esau. The Amalekites first appear in the bible when they attacked the Israelites on their way to the Promised Land. They attacked the stragglers at the rear, killing women and children.

> **Genesis 36:15** These were the chiefs among Esau's descendants: The sons of Eliphaz the firstborn of Esau: Chiefs Teman, Omar, Zepho, Kenaz, 16 Korah, Gatam and Amalek. These were the chiefs descended from Eliphaz in Edom; they were grandsons of Adah.

> **Exodus 17:8** The Amalekites came and attacked the Israelites at Rephidim. 9 Moses said to Joshua, 'Choose some of our men and go out to fight the Amalekites. Tomorrow I will stand on top of the hill with the staff of God in my hands.' 10 So Joshua fought the Amalekites as Moses had ordered, and Moses, Aaron and Hur went to the top of the hill. 13 So Joshua overcame the Amalekite army with the sword. 14 Then YHWH said to Moses, 'Write this on a scroll as some-thing to be remembered and make sure that Joshua hears it, because I will completely blot out the name of Amalek from under heaven.' 15 Moses built an altar and called it YHWH is my Banner. 16 He said, 'Because hands were lifted up against the throne of YHWH, YHWH will be at war against the Amalekites from generation to generation.'

The Amalekites inhabited the Negev – the southern part of modern Israel, and up to the eastern border of Egypt – what we now call the Sinai Peninsula.

> **Numbers 13:29** The Amalekites live in the Negev; the Hittites, Jebusites and Amorites live in the hill country; and the Canaanites live near the sea and along the Jordan.'

> **1 Samuel 15:7** Then Saul attacked the Amalekites all the way from Havilah to Shur, near the eastern border of Egypt.

King Saul was told by YHWH (through the prophet, Samuel) to completely destroy the Amalekites – however, Saul thought he knew better and spared their king and the best of the live-stock.

> **1 Samuel 15:1** Samuel said to Saul, 'I am the one YHWH sent to anoint you king over his people Israel; so listen now to the message from YHWH. 2 This is what YHWH Almighty says: "<u>I will punish the Amalekites for what they did to Israel when they waylaid them as they came up from Egypt</u>. 3 Now go, attack the Amalekites and totally destroy all that belongs to them. Do not spare them; put to death men and women, children and infants, cattle and sheep, camels and donkeys."' 4 So Saul summoned the men and mustered them at Telaim – two hundred thousand foot soldiers and ten thousand from Judah. 5 Saul went to the city of Amalek and set an ambush in the ravine. 6 Then he said to the Kenites, 'Go away, leave the Amalekites so that I do not destroy you along with them; for you showed kindness to all the Israelites when they came up out of Egypt.' So the Kenites moved away from the Amalekites.
>
> 7 <u>Then Saul attacked the Amalekites all the way from Havilah to Shur, near the eastern border of Egypt</u>. 8 He took Agag king of the Amalekites alive, and all his people he totally destroyed with the sword. 9 But Saul and the army spared Agag and the best of the sheep and cattle, the fat calves and lambs – everything that was good. These they were unwilling to destroy completely, but everything that was despised and weak they totally destroyed. 10 Then the word of YHWH came to Samuel: 11 'I regret that I have made Saul king, because he has turned away from me and has not carried out my instructions.' Samuel was angry, and he cried out to YHWH all that night.

YHWH having promised (in Exodus 17:14) to *'completely blot out the name of Amalek from under heaven'* and Saul having (eventually) carried out their destruction, it is hardly surprising that we no longer hear of Amalek today. The Amalekites have disappeared, but in the area they previously inhabited we still have some entrenched enemies of Israel.

Known originally as *Ansar Bait al-Maqdis*, they pledged allegiance to ISIS in 2014 and are known today as Sinai Province (of the ISIS caliphate – *Wilayat Sinai* in Arabic). They have successfully carried out attacks on Egyptian government troops and have fired rockets at the city of Eilat in Israel.

Does this mean that Egypt itself should be included among the conspirators? The prophet Joel mentions Egypt:

Joel 3:19 But <u>Egypt will be desolate</u>, Edom a desert waste, <u>because of violence done to the people of Judah</u>, in whose land they shed innocent blood.

Isaiah also gives a very detailed prophecy against Egypt:

Isaiah 19:12 Where are your wise men now? Let them show you and make known what YHWH Almighty has planned against Egypt. 13 The officials of Zoan have become fools, the leaders of Memphis are deceived; the cornerstones of her peoples have led Egypt astray. 14 YHWH has poured into them a spirit of dizziness; they make Egypt stagger in all that she does, as a drunkard staggers around in his vomit. 15 There is nothing Egypt can do – head or tail, palm branch or reed.

16 <u>In that day the Egyptians will become weaklings. They will shudder with fear at the uplifted hand that YHWH Almighty raises against them</u>. 17 And <u>the land of Judah will bring terror to the Egyptians; everyone to whom Judah is mentioned will be terrified</u>, because of what YHWH Almighty is planning against them.

18 In that day five cities in Egypt will speak the language of Canaan <u>and swear allegiance to YHWH Almighty</u>. One of them will be called the City of the Sun.

19 <u>In that day there will be an altar to YHWH in the heart of Egypt, and a monument to YHWH at its border</u>. 20 It will be a sign and witness to YHWH Almighty in the land of Egypt. When <u>they cry out to YHWH because of their oppressors, he will send them a saviour and defender, and he will rescue them. 21 So YHWH will make himself known to the Egyptians, and in that day they will acknowledge YHWH. They will worship with sacrifices and grain offerings; they will make vows to YHWH and keep them</u>. 22 YHWH will strike Egypt with a plague; he will strike them and heal them. <u>They will turn to YHWH, and he will respond to their pleas and heal them</u>.

23 In that day there will be a highway from Egypt to Assyria. The Assyrians will go to Egypt and the Egyptians to Assyria. <u>The Egyptians and Assyrians will worship together</u>. 24 In that day Israel will be the third, along with Egypt and Assyria, a blessing on the earth. 25 YHWH Almighty will bless them, saying, 'Blessed be Egypt my people, Assyria my handiwork, and Israel my in-heritance.'

The Egyptians will *'become weaklings, they will shudder with fear … the land of Judah will bring terror to the Egyptians; everyone to whom Judah is mentioned will be terrified.'* It seems like Egypt is definitely included among the hostile neighbours who will attack Israel! By the way, the City of the Sun in verse 18 (ancient *Heliopolis*), is now the *Ayn Shams* suburb of Cairo.

However, there is no mention of the Egyptians fleeing – even though they are terrified – instead they will *'turn to YHWH, and he will respond to their pleas and heal them.'* *'YHWH will make himself known to the Egyptians, and in that day they will acknowledge YHWH. They will worship … YHWH.'*

Psalm 83:18 'Let them know that you, whose name is YHWH – that you alone are the Most High over all the earth.'

As we said in Chapter 4, God's purpose in all of this conflict is that the Arab and Muslim nations will come to know him as Lord.

Ezekiel 28:26 [A prophecy against Sidon = Lebanon] [Jacob] will live in safety when I inflict punishment on all their neighbours who maligned them. <u>Then they will know that I am YHWH their God.</u>"'

While we are considering Egypt, the prophecies concerning her could also apply to the Sudan – especially now that Sudan and South Sudan are two separate countries. In the time of the Pharaohs Sudan was part of Egypt – during the New Kingdom period (1500 BC – 1070 BC) – and in more modern times, for more than a hundred years, was again part of Egypt – from 1821 until Sudan gained independence in 1956.

Sudan is an Arab Islamic state (Ishmaelite) that was previously vehemently opposed to Israel's existence, but – after signing the Abraham Accords in January 2021 – fully joined in February 2023. Unfortunately, in April 2023 a civil war broke out once again, so that the relationship with Israel is currently on hold. Sudan is presently a barrier to any African *aliyah* – of the Igbo, Lemba, Tutsi, etc. The prophecies against Ishmael and Egypt could well apply also to Sudan.

Amalekites – summary:

1. The Amalekites were a part of the Edomites – Amalek being the son of Eliphaz the son of Esau. Like the Philistines they were completely destroyed by Israel. There are no Amalekites in existence today.

2. They lived in the area of the southern Negev and what we now know as the Sinai Peninsula. In that area today we still see a dedicated enemy of Israel, originally calling themselves *Ansar Bait al-Maqdis.* They joined ISIS in 2014, now calling themselves *Wilayat Sinai* (Sinai Province).

3. Being part of Egyptian territory, does this mean Egypt are included in the attacking force? They are certainly included anyway as an Arab nation (*Ishmaelites*) bordering Israel – one of Israel's *'malicious neighbours.'*

4. Egypt is featured in prophecy from Isaiah (19) saying specifically that the Egyptians will *'shudder with fear'*, that *'Judah will bring terror to the Egyptians.'*

5. Unlike others in this conflict, Egyptians will not flee, but will *'turn to YHWH' 'and swear allegiance to YHWH Almighty.'*

6. Sudan could well be included in these prophecies, having been part of Egypt in ancient times and again in modern times from 1821-1956. The prophesied *'highway'* from Africa will probably pass through Sudan as well as Egypt.

13 – Meet the Neighbours: Assyria

Psalm 83:8 Even Assyria has joined them to reinforce Lot's descendants.

The Assyrians are another people who no longer exist as a nation, although there are still around one million Assyrian people – scattered throughout the Middle East and living in USA, Europe, etc. These are mostly members of the Assyrian Church of the East, the Chaldean Catholic Church, the Syriac Orthodox Church and the Syriac Catholic Church.

Israel is hardly likely to be attacked by Assyrian Christians, so who then, is being referred to as Assyria in Asaph's **Psalm 83** prophecy?

The area originally occupied by the once great nation of Assyria would today be the area of central Iraq – the original capital city of Ashur (also the name of their god) lies a little west of the Tigris river – but would also extend into present day Iran.

Southern Iraq today is mostly ruled by pro-Iranian Shi'ite militias, so coming more and more under the control of Iran. In the past they have been a continual enemy of Israel – declaring war in 1948 and sending an Iraqi Expeditionary Force of 18,000 men – though with little result.

They participated in the *Six Day War* against Israel in 1967, though arrived at the front too late to engage! In the Yom Kippur War in 1973 they sent 60,000 troops and 100 aircraft, but did not perform well. During the 1991 Gulf War Iraq fired 42 Scud missiles at Israel.

I was actually in Jerusalem just after the ceasefire and stayed in what had just recently been the *'sealed room'* of an apartment in the city centre. The Israelis had been prepared for a gas attack from Iraq, issuing gas masks to their population. My host peeled the tape off the keyhole and removed a blanket covering the window, before showing me into the room.

Technically, Iraq is still at war with Israel.

We have already looked at the prophecies foretelling the destruction of Iran (the Elamites). Any co-ordinated attack against Israel is most likely to involve Iran. Three of the prophesied participants – Hezbollah, in Lebanon; Hamas, in the Gaza Strip, and Syria – are supplied, trained and controlled by Iran.

Iran are rapidly heading towards having a significant nuclear capability – enough to be a serious threat to Israel. They continue to develop and test long-range missiles, capable of carrying a nuclear warhead to Israel.

Both Iraq and Iran will be involved in the attack.

Assyria – summary:

1. Assyria are no longer a nation today – represented by around one million people scattered around the Middle East and around the world – mostly members of various Assyrian Christian denominations – and certainly not hostile to Israel.

2. The area once occupied by Assyria today corresponds to Iraq and also Iran.

3. Arab Iraq have been long-time enemies of Israel – participating in every major war against Israel and also firing missiles against her in the 1991 Gulf War.

4. Iran, as we have already discussed, have threatened many times to *'wipe Israel off the map.'* – very much in line with the threat of Psalm 83:4. They are rapidly moving forward in their development of nuclear weapon capability – despite US and international opposition.

So, the attacking nations are identified:

Psalm 83/Isaiah 17   Today

Moab and Ammon	Jordan
the Ishmaelites	Saudi Arabia (plus)
the Hagrites (Hagarenes)	Syria
Damascus (Isaiah 17)	Syria
Byblos/Tyre	Lebanon
Philistia	Gaza Strip (Palestinians)
the tents of Edom	Palestinians
Amalek	Sinai Province (ISIS)/ Egypt?/Sudan?
(Isaiah 19)	Egypt/Sudan
Assyria	Iran/Iraq

14 – The 'everlasting hatred'

The Hebrew prophets talk about something they call the *'ancient hostility'* – Hebrew: *'olam ebah'*, or *'everlasting hatred.'* This began with Ishmael, who mocked his younger brother – probably because he was jealous of Isaac being the child of promise:

> **Genesis 21:8** The child grew and was weaned, and on the day Isaac was weaned Abraham held a great feast. 9 But <u>Sarah saw that the son whom Hagar the Egyptian had borne to Abraham was mocking</u>, 10 and she said to Abraham, 'Get rid of that slave woman and her son, for that woman's son will never share in the inheritance with my son Isaac.'

The apostle Paul refers to this hatred (persecution) in his letter to the Galatians:

> **Galatians 4:28** Now you, brothers and sisters, like Isaac, are children of promise. 29 At that time <u>the son born according to the flesh</u> [Ishmael] <u>persecuted the son born by the power of the Spirit</u> [Isaac].

It is the same now!

The hatred continued with Esau – the man who despised his own inheritance and the blessing of YHWH, selling his birthright to Jacob (Israel) in exchange for some red lentil stew – and has continued to ferment down through the centuries and the generations.

> **Genesis 27:41** <u>Esau held a grudge against Jacob</u> because of the blessing his father had given him. He said to himself, 'The days of mourning for my father are near; then <u>I will kill my brother Jacob</u>.'

> **Ezekiel 35:5** "'Because you [Edom] harboured an <u>ancient hostility</u> and delivered the Israelites over to the sword at the time of their calamity, the time their punishment reached its climax, 6 therefore as surely as I live, declares the Sovereign YHWH, I will give you over to bloodshed and it will pursue you. Since you did not hate bloodshed, bloodshed will pursue you. 7 <u>I will make Mount Seir a desolate waste and cut off from it all who come</u>

and go. 8 I will fill your mountains with the slain; those killed by the sword will fall on your hills and in your valleys and in all your ravines. 9 <u>I will make you desolate for ever; your towns will not be inhabited</u>. Then you will know that I am YHWH.

Amos 1:11 This is what YHWH says: 'For three sins of Edom, even for four, I will not relent. Because he pursued his brother with a sword and slaughtered the women of the land, because <u>his anger raged continually and his fury flamed unchecked</u>, 12 I will send fire on Teman that will consume the fortresses of Bozrah.'

The Edomites (Palestinians) of Judaea and Samaria – the so-called, 'West Bank' – harbour an *'ancient hostility'* towards Israel, resulting in their continued assault on Jewish targets within Israel and their failure to acknowledge Israel's right to exist, or to make any move towards peace with Israel. They have rejected every offer of an independent state for themselves and make it clear that their goal is the elimination of Israel. They pass on this *'everlasting hatred'* from generation to generation.

Ezekiel 25 <u>A prophecy against Philistia</u>

15 'This is what the Sovereign YHWH says: "Because the Philistines acted in vengeance and took revenge with malice in their hearts, and with <u>ancient hostility</u> sought to destroy Judah, 16 therefore this is what the Sovereign YHWH says: I am about to stretch out my hand against the Philistines, and I will wipe out the Kerethites and destroy those remaining along the coast. 17 I will carry out great vengeance on them and punish them in my wrath. <u>Then they will know that I am YHWH</u>, when I take vengeance on them."'

Like the ancient Philistines, the 'Palestinians' of the Gaza Strip also harbour an *'ancient hostility'* towards Israel, resulting in their continued assault against Israel and Jews. Hamas – the terrorist group controlling the Gaza Strip, along with Palestinian Islamic Jihad – wants to rid the world of Israel. They have zero interest in any peace deal with Israel.

In their charter – which you can read here* (2nd paragraph) – the organisation states: *"Israel will exist and will continue to exist until Islam will obliterate it, just as it obliterated others before it."*

*avalon.law.yale.edu/20th_century/hamas.asp

We can see this in the Palestinian education system today – both under Hamas, in Gaza, and the Palestinian authority (PLO/Fatah) in the so-called West Bank. Children are taught that Israel and the Jews are evil aggressors who are eager to kill them. Maps labelled *'Palestine'* depict the whole area of Israel. Summer youth camps train young people to become suicide bombers and terrorists. Money received as humanitarian aid is used to pay terrorists and their families. Truly, their *'anger rages continually and their fury flames unchecked'* (**Amos 1:11**).

This hatred – this *'ancient hostility'* – was evident during the re-building of Jerusalem in the time of Ezra and Nehemiah:

Nehemiah 2:19 But when Sanballat the Horonite, Tobiah the Ammonite official and Geshem the Arab heard about it, they mocked and ridiculed us. 'What is this you are doing?' they asked.

Nehemiah 4:7 But when Sanballat, Tobiah, the Arabs, the Ammonites and the people of Ashdod heard that the repairs to Jerusalem's walls had gone ahead and that the gaps were being closed, they were very angry.

Nehemiah 6:1 [Further opposition to the rebuilding] When word came to Sanballat, Tobiah, Geshem the Arab and the rest of our enemies that I had rebuilt the wall and not a gap was left in it – though up to that time I had not set the doors in the gates.

The hatred extends to all the Arab nations surrounding Israel. Their hostility is really aimed against YHWH, the God of Israel, though it is expressed in action against Jews and the State of Israel. This also explains why these nations have embraced another God, Allah, and the religion of Islam, whose hatred of Jews and Israel is embodied in the Quran.

Genesis 16:11 The angel of YHWH also said to [Hagar]: You are now pregnant and you will give birth to a son. You shall name him Ishmael, for YHWH has heard of your misery. 12 He will be a wild donkey of a man; his hand will be against everyone and everyone's hand against him, and he will live in hostility towards all his brothers.'

Genesis 25:17 [Ishmael] breathed his last and died, and he was gathered to his people. 18 His descendants settled in the area from Havilah to Shur, near the eastern border of Egypt, as you go towards Ashur. And <u>they lived in hostility towards all the tribes related to them</u>.

The *'ancient hostility'* affects all of the children of Ishmael – i.e. the Arab people.

Psalm 83:2 For behold, Your enemies make an uproar,
And <u>those who hate You</u> have exalted themselves. (NASV)

Isaiah 41:11-12 '<u>All who rage against you</u> will surely be ashamed and disgraced; those who oppose you will be as nothing and perish. Though you search for your enemies, you will not find them. Those who wage war against you will be as nothing at all.

Not only the Arab nations, but this hostility is also common to all Islamic nations – no more so than Iran! Over and over Iranian leaders and generals threaten that they will one day soon destroy Israel. The *'everlasting hatred'* continues!

In contrast, the rapidly growing Christian church in Iran are not only embracing the Jewish Messiah, but also his people, the Jews, and Israel – so there *is* a way to destroy the power of this *'everlasting hatred'* – through a relationship with Yeshua/ Jesus.

'Everlasting hatred' – summary:

1. At the age of thirteen Ishmael was discovered mocking his baby brother – he and his mother, Hagar, were immediately expelled from the family. Paul refers to Ishmael *'persecuting'* Isaac. (Galatians 4:29)

2. Esau despised his birthright and sold it to Jacob (Israel) – but then hated him for it and wanted to kill him.

3. That *'ancient hostility'* has been passed on down the generations of Edomites/Idumeans/Palestinians to this day.

4. Ezekiel applies this *'ancient hostility'* to Philistia, also – today represented by Edomite Gaza.

5. The *'everlasting hatred'* extends to all of the Arab nations – Ishmaelites (Genesis 16:11,12; 25:17,18) and indeed to all the Islamic nations, too – especially today to Iran.

15 – The unholy alliance

There is currently quite a serious series of wars taking place in the Middle East, being waged in different areas of the region. Iran – a totally Shi'ite nation – are backing Hezbollah (a Shi'ite militia) and Hamas (Sunni, Moslem Brotherhood), and also have their own Revolutionary Guard units (IRGC) operating in Syria in support of President Assad (Alawite Muslim) and fighting against the opposition rebel forces of Al Nusra (Salafi) and the Free Syrian Army (Sunni). ISIS (Sunni) are in there as well, though their influence has now been greatly reduced.

In Yemen a war has been ongoing since 2015, involving Houthi rebels, – backed by Iran – who have taken control of the capital, Sa'ana. They are fighting the Hadi Government forces, based in Aden, who are supported by Saudi Arabia. Other forces involved include the *Southern Transitional Council* (a separatist movement, who now control Aden), Ansar al-Sharia/Al Quaeda in the Arabian Peninsula (Sunni) and ISIS/ISIL (Sunni).

Essentially the civil war in Yemen is a proxy war being fought between Shi'ite Iran and Sunni/Wahabi Saudi Arabia, through their specific proxies. The war is significant because it highlights the great divide between Sunni and Shia Muslims, which can erupt – and has done in the past – into full scale war between these two main sects of Islam.

The *Six Hour War* represents an unholy alliance between Sunni and Shia, in order to destroy their common enemy – Israel. The strength and durability of such an alliance would depend very much on how quickly they could achieve their common objectives. Any setback to these – for instance, such as Israel quickly gaining the upper hand in the conflict – and the fragile unity could unravel very quickly.

From the Hebrew prophets we know that this alliance is not going to achieve its objective of destroying Israel – in fact, Isaiah gives us a clue as to how this might come about:

Isaiah 17:14 <u>In the evening, sudden terror! Before the morning, they are gone!</u> This is the portion of those who loot us, the lot of those who plunder us.

In other words, a sudden terrible attack against Israel in the evening – such as a nuclear missile, more likely series of missiles – fired at Israel by Iran, or possibly Syria. But before morning – in other words, within a few hours – the threat is over and Israel go onto the offensive.

How might this come about? And what effect might it have upon the conflict? Israeli technology is some of the most advanced in the world – particularly in the areas of high tech and computing/ cyber warfare.

Stuxnet comes to mind – a malicious computer worm developed by Israel, in co-operation with the USA – which in 2010 attacked over 200,000 Iranian computer systems – in particular those systems controlling their nuclear centrifuges – causing them to spin out of control and tear themselves apart. *Stuxnet* destroyed almost one fifth of Iran's centrifuges and physically damaged over 1,000 computers.

Israeli technologists have a lot of experience in missile guidance software and it is only natural to expect that they are working hard to intercept enemy technology and software. In my novel, *'In Six Hours'*, I describe an IDF unit operating from Ha Technion University in Haifa, hacking into Iranian and Syrian missile software and re-writing it so as to leave room for their own additional code.

I studied *Computing and Information Systems* myself at the University of Ulster, just outside Belfast. One of my classes was on machine code programming. I know that much of today's software is written with the help of software assistance, but these tend to produce code which is wasteful of memory and can usually be re-written more efficiently – leaving memory available which can accommodate extra code.

One of our projects was to write a simple routine to input three pieces of information and then to print that information out. Most of my class wrote the same routine three times over, whereas I wrote one routine and called it three times, using different parameters. It took a little bit more thought and application, but resulted in much more efficient code.

To be honest, my lecturer didn't deign to give me any credit for using my intelligence and seemed to take my work as some sort of challenge, with the result that he ignored me for the rest of the term!

Israel's scientific and military establishment are of a different calibre from my lecturer, thankfully, and select the brightest and best to work on these problems. I would not be surprised to find that they had anticipated and infiltrated the enemy's systems to the extent that they can divert them, if they are aimed at an Israeli target.

In my fiction that is just what 'Potter' and his team achieve, helped by up-to-date intelligence being fed to them from several friendly sources – writing their own code into the enemy software.

They follow a similar procedure to how the existing Israeli *Iron Dome* and *Iron Beam* missile defence systems work at present. When a hostile missile is launched, *Iron Dome* radar will detect the launch and determine exactly where that rocket will land, taking into account weather factors, etc. If it is not a threat – i.e. it will land in a field, or the desert – no action is taken.

If a population centre is threatened then the system launches an expensive *Tamir* missile to take out the enemy rocket. *Iron Beam* operates in the same way, except it fires a high intensity laser beam at the incoming rocket – much less expensive than a $50,000 missile!

Israel have other missile defence systems to defend against long range missile attacks – *Arrow 2* and *3* and also *David's Sling* – but diverting the enemy's missile to *'return to sender'* halfway through its trajectory seems a very likely scenario. If there is no time to do that – because the missile was launched close by – e.g. from Syrian territory – then the missile would be diverted to the nearest enemy target, or even into the sea.

Even if the turnaround comes about in some other way – perhaps simply miraculously, by the hand of God – the failure to disable Israel will put quite a strain on a wholly unnatural and unstable alliance and it would not take much for Iran and Saudi Arabia (possibly Egypt, also) to change targets and fire upon one another in their anger and frustration.

You may think that Saudi Arabia are not in possession of nuclear missiles, but remember, they are close allies with fellow Sunni state, Pakistan – who definitely *do* possess nuclear missiles, in abundance. It is quite possible that Saudi Arabia may already have obtained a secret supply of these missiles in readiness for such a scenario!

In that case the war could quickly degenerate into an all-out Sunni/Shia war, in which both countries are devastated and reduced to a primitive state – leaving Israel to dominate and control the area and their own populations to flee from a potential nuclear holocaust. This would also open the prophesied '*Highway from Assyria*' for the ten tribes to return home to Israel.

Just as YHWH did with the ancient Moabites, Ammonites and Edomites in Jehoshaphat's time, so He is able to do again today with the contemporary enemies of Israel. Israel would then find themselves without any viable enemies – except possibly, Turkey, whose involvement is not mentioned in this conflict, but may well have a role in a later, and final, one.

Unholy alliance – summary:

1.   The two main divisions of Islam have been divided since the earliest days of the followers of Mohammed.

2.   Sunni and Shia are today fighting proxy wars in Syria, Iraq and in Yemen – backed either by Iran, or Saudi Arabia.

3.   An alliance between these two branches can only be short-lived – any setback to their plans and the alliance could unravel very quickly, pitting Iran and Saudi Arabia, Egypt, etc. against one another once again.

4.   Saudi Arabia are not regarded as a nuclear power, but they are still in a position to secretly acquire nuclear missiles from their Sunni brothers in Pakistan.

5.   An all-out war between Sunni and Shia Islam would devastate all of the countries involved, leaving Israel in control and the highway from Assyria open for the Ingathering.

16 – The fear of YHWH

In my fictional series depicting these events – *'In Six Hours …
the world changed'* and *'In One Hour … Babylon will fall'* I
painted a scenario where Israel were responding to an all-out
attack on them from all sides, but finding it difficult to catch up with
their fleeing enemies. The fear of God had fallen upon their
enemies as Moses promised:

> **Genesis 35:5** Then [Jacob/Israel] set out, and the terror of God
> fell on the towns all around them so that no one pursued them.

> **Deuteronomy 2:25** This very day I will begin to put the
> terror and fear of you on all the nations under heaven. They
> will hear reports of you and will tremble and be in anguish
> because of you.'

> **Deuteronomy 11:25** No one will be able to stand against
> you. YHWH your God, as he promised you, will put the terror
> and fear of you on the whole land, wherever you go.

> **Deuteronomy 28:7** YHWH will grant that the enemies who
> rise up against you will be defeated before you. They will come
> at you from one direction but flee from you in seven.

I want to show that this is a realistic expectation. There are
several examples in scripture where similar events happened
– but such events also took place in the not too distant past
in modern Israel.

The first example is where King Saul's son, Jonathan, and
his armour bearer climbed up a cliff, at a place called Michmash,
in full view of the mocking Philistines. At the time, out of the
whole Israelite army, only Saul and Jonathan possessed swords!

> **I Samuel 14:12** So Jonathan said to his armour-bearer, "Climb
> up after me; YHWH has given them into the hand of Israel."
> 13 Jonathan climbed up, using his hands and feet, with his
> armour-bearer right behind him. The Philistines fell before
> Jonathan, and his armour-bearer followed and killed behind him.
> 14 In that first attack Jonathan and his armour-bearer killed some

twenty men in an area of about half an acre. 15 <u>Then panic struck the whole army—those in the camp and field, and those in the outposts and raiding parties</u>—and the ground shook. <u>It was a panic sent by God.</u> 16 Saul's lookouts at Gibeah in Benjamin saw the army <u>melting away in all directions</u>.

In this case God used one man with a sword – plus his armour-bearer, probably using a captured sword – to initially kill twenty of the enemy, but the effect of their attack brought panic to the whole Philistine army – a panic sent by God – so that they *'melted away in all directions.'*

The second example is from King Jehoshaphat, when Judah was about to be attacked by the combined armies of the Moabites, Ammonites and the Edomites:

2 Chronicles 20:1 After this, the Moabites and Ammonites with some of the Meunites came to wage war against Jehoshaphat.

2 Some people came and told Jehoshaphat, 'A vast army is coming against you from Edom, from the other side of the Dead Sea. It is already in Hazezon Tamar' (that is, En Gedi). 3 Alarmed, Jehoshaphat resolved to enquire of YHWH, and he proclaimed a fast for all Judah. 4 The people of Judah came together to seek help from YHWH; indeed, they came from every town in Judah to seek him.

5 Then Jehoshaphat stood up in the assembly of Judah and Jerusalem at the temple of YHWH in the front of the new courtyard 6 and said: 'YHWH, the God of our ancestors, are you not the God who is in heaven? You rule over all the kingdoms of the nations. Power and might are in your hand, and no one can withstand you. 7 Our God, did you not drive out the inhabitants of this land before your people Israel and give it for ever to the descendants of Abraham your friend? 8 They have lived in it and have built in it a sanctuary for your Name, saying, 9 "If calamity comes upon us, whether the sword of judgment, or plague or famine, we will stand in your presence before this temple that bears your Name and will cry out to you in our distress, and you will hear us and save us." 10 'But now here are men from Ammon, Moab and Mount Seir, whose territory you would not allow Israel to invade when they came from Egypt; so they turned away from them and did not destroy them. 11 See how they are repaying us by coming to drive us out of the possession you gave us as an inheritance. 12 Our God, will you not judge them? For we have no power to face this vast army that is attacking us. We do not know what to do, but our eyes are on you.'

13 All the men of Judah, with their wives and children and little ones, stood there before YHWH.

14 Then the Spirit of YHWH came on Jahaziel son of Zechariah, the son of Benaiah, the son of Jeiel, the son of Mattaniah, a Levite and descendant of Asaph, as he stood in the assembly. 15 He said: 'Listen, King Jehoshaphat and all who live in Judah and Jerusalem! This is what YHWH says to you: "Do not be afraid or discouraged because of this vast army. For the battle is not yours, but God's. 16 Tomorrow march down against them. They will be climbing up by the Pass of Ziz, and you will find them at the end of the gorge in the Desert of Jeruel. 17 You will not have to fight this battle. Take up your positions; stand firm and see the deliverance YHWH will give you, Judah and Jerusalem. Do not be afraid; do not be discouraged. Go out to face them tomorrow, and YHWH will be with you."'

18 Jehoshaphat bowed down with his face to the ground, and all the people of Judah and Jerusalem fell down in worship before YHWH. 19 Then some Levites from the Kohathites and Korahites stood up and praised YHWH, the God of Israel, with a very loud voice.

20 Early in the morning they left for the Desert of Tekoa. As they set out, Jehoshaphat stood and said, 'Listen to me, Judah and people of Jerusalem! Have faith in YHWH your God and you will be upheld; have faith in his prophets and you will be successful.' 21 After consulting the people, Jehoshaphat appointed men to sing to YHWH and to praise him for the splendour of his holiness as they went out at the head of the army, saying: 'Give thanks to YHWH, for his love endures for ever.'

22 As they began to sing and praise, YHWH set ambushes against the men of Ammon and Moab and Mount Seir who were invading Judah, and they were defeated. 23 The Ammonites and Moabites rose up against the men from Mount Seir to destroy and annihilate them. After they finished slaughtering the men from Seir, they helped to destroy one another.

24 When the men of Judah came to the place that overlooks the desert and looked towards the vast army, they saw only dead bodies lying on the ground; no one had escaped. 25 So Jehoshaphat and his men went to carry off their plunder, and they found among them a great amount of equipment and clothing and also articles of value – more than they could take away. There was so much plunder that it took three days to collect it. 26 On the fourth day they assembled in the Valley of Berakah, where they praised YHWH. This is why it is called the Valley of Berakah [praise] to this day.

27 Then, led by Jehoshaphat, all the men of Judah and Jeru-salem returned joyfully to Jerusalem, for YHWH had given them cause to rejoice over their enemies. 28 They entered Jerusalem and went to the temple of YHWH with harps and lyres and trumpets.

29 <u>The fear of God came on all the surrounding kingdoms when they heard</u> how YHWH had fought against the enemies of Israel. 30 And the kingdom of Jehoshaphat was at peace, for his God had given him rest on every side.

This is an amazing story – firstly Jehoshaphat, realising Judah did not have the strength to defeat this *'vast army'* coming to attack them, called a fast throughout Israel and prayed for help from YHWH. YHWH answered through the prophet, Jahaziel son of Zechariah, telling the Israelites, *'You will not have to fight this battle!'*

Sure enough as Judah worshipped YHWH the Moabites and Ammonites turned against the Edomites and destroyed them, then turned against one another and every last one was wiped out! All Judah had to do was spend three days collecting all the spoil from the defeated armies!

As a result of this battle *'the fear of God came on all the surrounding kingdoms when they heard'* about this event! Surely the same God can do this again for Israel in their hour of greatest need?

In fact, he did just that during the War of Independence in 1948. The town of Safad, or Tzefat – the *'highest city in Israel'* at 900m above sea level – was a mainly Arab town (12,000 population) during Israel's War of Independence. The Jewish population of Safad (1,700) was almost entirely made up of religious scholars, Yeshiva students and elderly men – NOT men who could fight against their enemies.

When the British withdrew from Safad, 200 members of the Syrian-led *Arab Liberation Army,* aided by another 200 local Arab militiamen, attacked the Jewish Quarter, but were repelled by 200 men of the Haganah (Jewish forces), aided by a small platoon of Palmach commandos. It was an uphill struggle for the Jewish forces – fighting house to house each day and gaining little ground, with heavy casualties.

They asked Haganah command for reinforcements, but these were not forthcoming – all they received were a couple of locally made mortars, which the Jews had christened *'Davidkas'* – i.e. little Davids. These fired an explosive projectile which looked more like a mallet than a shell! As it tumbled through the air it made a whistling sound, though it was not a particularly effective weapon.

Next morning, after firing this weapon several times the night before, the Palmach prepared for more heavy house to house fighting. As they moved out they encountered no return fire and discovered that the 12,000 Arab residents (some estimate as many as 15,000) had fled the town overnight, believing a rumour – based on the strange whistling sound of the *Davidka* – that the Israelis had acquired the Atom bomb!

An irrational *'fear of God'* had come upon the Arab population. Among the 12,000 who fled Safad that night – never to return – was the family of current Palestinian Authority President, Mahmoud Abbas – a man who now takes the millions of dollars foolishly handed to him by the west and spends it on training terrorists and supporting the families of those guilty of murdering Jews!

Deuteronomy 11:24 Every place where you [Israel] set your foot will be yours: your territory will extend from the desert to Lebanon, and from the River Euphrates to the Mediterranean Sea. 25 No one will be able to stand against you. YHWH your God, as he promised you, will put the terror and fear of you on the whole land, wherever you go.

Jeremiah 49:2 But the days are coming," declares YHWH, "when I will sound the battle cry against Rabbah of the Ammonites; it will become a mound of ruins, and its surrounding villages will be set on fire. Then Israel will drive out those who drove her out," says YHWH.

5 I will bring terror on [the Ammonites] from all those around you," declares YHWH, YHWH Almighty. "Every one of you will be driven away, and no one will gather the fugitives.

Jeremiah 49:23 Concerning Damascus. "Hamath and Arpad are put to shame, For they have heard bad news; They are disheartened. There is anxiety by the sea, It cannot be calmed. 24 "Damascus has become helpless; She has turned away to flee, And panic has gripped her; Distress and pangs have taken hold of her Like a woman in childbirth. 25 "How the city of praise has not been deserted, The town of My joy! 26 "Therefore, her young men will fall in her streets, And all the men of war will be silenced in

<u>that day</u>," declares YHWH of hosts. 27 "<u>I will set fire to the wall of Damascus, And it will devour the fortified towers</u> of Ben-hadad."

Isaiah 19:16 <u>In that day</u> the Egyptians will become weaklings. <u>They will shudder with fear at the uplifted hand that YHWH Almighty raises against them</u>. 17 And <u>the land of Judah will bring terror to the Egyptians; everyone to whom Judah is mentioned will be terrified</u>, because of what YHWH Almighty is planning against them.

After Jacob's sons slaughtered the men of Shechem, Jacob moved all that he had to Bethel, '*and <u>the terror of God fell on the towns all around them</u> so that no one pursued them*'. (**Genesis 35:5**)

Later, Moses prophesied that, '*<u>YHWH … will put the terror and fear of you on the whole land</u>, wherever you go.*' (**Deuteronomy 11:25**)

Jeremiah repeated this in relation to the **Ammonites** – '<u>*I will bring terror on you from*</u> [Israel – v.2] *all those around you,*" declares YHWH, YHWH Almighty. "*Every one of you will be driven away.*' (**Jeremiah 49:5**) He repeats this regarding **Syria** in the same chapter: '*Damascus has become helpless; She has turned away to flee, and <u>panic has gripped her</u>; distress and pangs have taken hold of her like a woman in childbirth.*' (**Jeremiah 49:24**)

Isaiah applies the same result to **Egypt**: '*the Egyptians will become weaklings. 'They will shudder with fear … the land of Judah will bring terror to the Egyptians; everyone to whom Judah is mentioned will be terrified.*' (**Isaiah 19:16,17**)

After a possible failed Arab/Muslim nuclear attack upon Israel – '*before the morning, they are gone*' (**Isaiah 17:14**) – would it not be likely that their enemies would fully expect Israel to retaliate with nuclear weapons – especially if Israel have managed to divert their enemies' weapons, destroying cities like Damascus, as prophesied?

The fear of being slaughtered in revenge – no matter how unlikely an event from an Israeli point of view – could become a driving force causing these Arab populations to flee in terror, rather than face the expected wrath of Israel.

As I said at the start, Isaiah 17 and Psalm 83 prophesy that these attacking nations will become like *'chaff in the wind'*, like *'tumbleweed in a gale.'*

Isaiah 17:13 when He rebukes them they flee far away, <u>driven before the wind like chaff on the hills, like tumbleweed before a gale</u>

Psalm 83:13 <u>Make them like tumbleweed, my God, like chaff before the wind</u>. 14 As fire consumes the forest or a flame sets the mountains ablaze, 15 so pursue them with your tempest and terrify them with your storm.

Zechariah 12:2 'I am going to make Jerusalem <u>a cup that sends all the surrounding peoples reeling</u>.

6 'On that day I will make the clans of Judah like a brazier in a woodpile, like a flaming torch among sheaves. <u>They will consume all the surrounding peoples right and left</u>, but Jerusalem will remain intact in her place.

Ezekiel 28:23 Then you will know that I am YHWH. 24 '"<u>No longer will the people of Israel have malicious neighbours </u>who are painful briers and sharp thorns. Then they will know that I am the Sovereign YHWH.

26 They will live in safety <u>when I inflict punishment on all their neighbours who maligned them</u>. Then they will know that I am YHWH their God."

The fear of YHWH will cause them to flee – send them reeling, *'driven before the wind'*.

The fear of YHWH – summary:

1. YHWH used Saul's son, Jonathan – the only other man in Israel who possessed a sword – to bring the fear of YHWH into the Philistine camp.

2. Jehoshaphat prayed and YHWH answered through a prophet – *'the battle is YHWH's'.* Judah did not have to fight – the Moabites and Ammonites wiped out the Edomites, then destroyed one another. Then *'the fear of God came on all the surrounding kingdoms.'*

3. In 1948, in Safad – even though their fighters out-numbered the Jewish defenders 2:1 – the Arab population of 12,000+ fled the city overnight; the result of fear based on a rumour!

4. *'I will bring terror on you* [Ammon = Jordan] *... declares YHWH ... every one of you will be driven away'* (**Jeremiah 49:5)**

5. Egypt *'will shudder with fear'* and *'be terrified'* because of what YHWH raises against them. *'Judah will bring terror to the Egyptians'* (**Isaiah 19:16,17)**

6. What God did for Jacob, Jonathan, and for Jehoshaphat in the bible – and for Safad in 1948 – he can certainly do again for modern-day Israel.

7. The fear of YHWH will cause many of Israel's neigh-bours to flee – like *'chaff on the hills, like tumbleweed before a gale.' 'Jerusalem – a cup that sends all the surrounding peoples reeling.'*

8. No more malicious neighbours!

17 – Ripples around the world

Micah 4:11 But now <u>many nations are gathered against you.</u> <u>They say, "Let her be defiled, let our eyes gloat over Zion!"</u> 12 But they do not know the thoughts of YHWH; they do not understand his plan, that he has gathered them like sheaves to the threshing floor. 13 "Rise and thresh, Daughter Zion, for I will give you horns of iron; I will give you hooves of bronze, and <u>you will break to pieces many nations."</u> <u>You will devote their ill-gotten gains to YHWH, their wealth to YHWH of all the earth</u>.

Israel will need time to recover from this war. There will be many dead and injured, towns and military facilities damaged, etc. But after this war Israel will end up in control of the Middle East, in control of the wealth of her former enemies. Micah refers to Israel having control of *'their ill-gotten gains ... their wealth.'*

This war will not only affect Israel and the Middle East, those effects will be felt around the world. Israel's status, though initially uncertain because of taking on an influx of millions of immigrants – the Second Exodus, the Ingathering of the ten tribes – will soon stabilise, because of their innate capacity to recover quickly from adversity and also their well known problem-solving abilities.

Only a nation such as Israel could hope to deal with an *aliyah* of perhaps one hundred million people over a short period of time, coupled with recovering from a devastating war *and* re-building the infrastructure of the former nations around them – now their responsibility.

The short term affect would probably be a fall in the world's stock markets. With Saudi Arabia and Iran effectively out of the picture there would undoubtedly be a great deal of uncertainty about oil supplies. I imagine Israel would be quick to take control here and to get pipelines and oilfields operational as quickly as possible. The main problem, I would think, would be encouraging investors to finance this and other projects in the new Israel.

The Kurds, who control an area of oil supplies – the oil-fields around Kirkuk – would no doubt be very willing to work together with Israel to accomplish this. In the past – 1935-48 – the Kirkuk–Haifa oil pipeline ran from the Kurdish Kirkuk oil-field, through Jordan and the British Mandate, to the Mediterranean coast at Haifa. Needless to say, this pipeline ceased to function after the birth of the State of Israel. The USA actually proposed re-opening this pipeline in a telegram to the Israeli government in 2003.

The Kirkuk-Banias oil pipeline was commissioned in 1952 and was operational until the early 1990s, when the Gulf War put an end to operations. It terminated at the port of Banias in northern Syria. There were proposals to re-open the pipeline, but the current civil war in Syria has resulted in at least two of the pumping stations falling into ISIS' hands for a time.

The previously proposed – but never completed – Iran-Iraq-Syria gas pipeline could easily be developed, bringing gas to the Mediterranean coast, where it would be much easier to ship it to the US, etc. – or to pipe it on to Europe. An oil pipeline could be built along the same route and ships would no longer have to make the round trip to the Persian Gulf for oil.

Israelis are known for a *'can do'* attitude to things that might seem difficult – so these projects are distinct possibilities, especially when Israel will have an abundance of manpower due to the *aliyah*.

At the moment Israel is enjoying a very positive relationship with the USA. However, if we look at the current situation in the United States – it is apparent that the USA has become a very divided country.

I am reminded of Jeremiah's words:

> **Jeremiah 51:8** Wail over her! Get balm for her pain; <u>perhaps she can be healed</u>. 9 '"<u>We would have healed Babylon, but she cannot be healed</u>; let us leave her and each go to our own land, for her judgment reaches to the skies, it rises as high as the heavens."

There are many believers in the US, who believe in interceding for their country – and they are right to do so! I believe the election of Donald Trump – rough diamond that he is! – was in answer to those prayers! But these verses keep echoing in my head, *'We would have healed her, but she cannot be healed!'* It seems to me that, no matter who is president, the breach in the country is only getting wider.

Obama was a disaster, Hilary Clinton would have been even worse – Biden is currently fully supportive of Israel. But in future there may come a complete reversal in US policy toward Israel.

Already Iran is well down the road towards nuclear weapons capability – which could bring about the confidence in Israel's enemies to launch this attack. Does America have one more year, or five more?

Really, this is a subject for another book – actually, one I have already written! – *'The Whore and her Mother'* – but it needs to be at least touched on here.

If the USA should turn away from Israel, and facilitate Iran gaining a nuclear capability, then America could bear a grave responsibility for not only many thousands of deaths in Israel, but for possibly millions of deaths throughout the Middle East.

Jeremiah 51:24 'Before your eyes I will repay Babylon and all who live in Babylonia for all the wrong they have done in Zion,' declares YHWH.

Jeremiah 50:18 Therefore this is what YHWH Almighty, the God of Israel, says: 'I will punish the king of Babylon and his land as I punished the king of Assyria. 19 But I will bring Israel back to their own pasture, and they will graze on Carmel and Bashan [Golan Heights]; their appetite will be satisfied on the hills of Ephraim and Gilead [Jordan].

33 This is what YHWH Almighty says: 'The people of Israel are oppressed, and the people of Judah as well. All their captors hold them fast, refusing to let them go. 34 Yet their Redeemer is strong; YHWH Almighty is his name. He will vigorously defend their cause so that he may bring rest to their land, but unrest to those who live in Babylon.

It may soon be time for Israel to get out of Babylon!

Ripples around the world – summary:

1. War in the Middle East is going to have a negative effect on the world economy, but hopefully Israel will be able to restore confidence – and restore oil and gas supplies. It will require considerable manpower and investment.

2. The present cosy relationship with the USA may only have a short time to go. The country is so divided that it is almost inevitable that a hostile president will succeed to the White House in the near future. What then for Israel?

3. Renewing Iran's ability to develop nuclear weapons would only encourage these hostile nations to attempt to destroy Israel.

4. Could American policy in the Middle East lead to thousands of deaths in Israel? Millions across the region?

5. If that becomes a reality will it then be time for the Jews to flee Babylon? Jeremiah more than suggests this!

18 – The war still to come

While discussing the *Six Hour War* – an attack by the countries surrounding Israel – we need to also look briefly at another war which is prophesied in scripture. The two wars are similar in one respect – Israel against everyone else! – but different in many other ways.

This war is sometimes referred to by bible scholars as the Gog/Magog war and it is described by the prophet Ezekiel:

Ezekiel 38 The word of YHWH came to me: 2 'Son of man, set your face against Gog, of the land of Magog, the chief prince of Meshek and Tubal; prophesy against him 3 and say: "This is what the Sovereign YHWH says: I am against you, Gog, chief prince of Meshek and Tubal. 4 I will turn you around, put hooks in your jaws and bring you out with your whole army – your horses, your horsemen fully armed, and a great horde with large and small shields, all of them brandishing their swords. 5 Persia, Cush and Put will be with them, all with shields and helmets, 6 also Gomer with all its troops, and Beth Togarmah from the far north with all its troops – the many nations with you.

7 "'Get ready; be prepared, you and all the hordes gathered about you, and take command of them. 8 After many days you will be called to arms. In future years you will invade a land that has recovered from war, whose people were gathered from many nations to the mountains of Israel, which had long been desolate. They had been brought out from the nations, and now all of them live in safety. 9 You and all your troops and the many nations with you will go up, advancing like a storm; you will be like a cloud covering the land.

10 "'This is what the Sovereign YHWH says: on that day thoughts will come into your mind and you will devise an evil scheme. 11 You will say, 'I will invade a land of unwalled villages; I will attack a peaceful and unsuspecting people – all of them living without walls and without gates and bars. 12 I will plunder and loot and turn my hand against the resettled ruins and the people gathered from the nations, rich in livestock and goods, living at the centre of the land [earth].' 13 Sheba and Dedan and the

merchants of Tarshish and all her villages will say to you, 'Have you come to plunder? Have you gathered your hordes to loot, to carry off silver and gold, to take away livestock and goods and to seize much plunder?'"

14 'Therefore, son of man, prophesy and say to Gog: "This is what the Sovereign YHWH says: in that day, <u>when my people Israel are living in safety</u>, will you not take notice of it? 15 <u>You will come from your place in the far north, you and many nations with you</u>, all of them riding on horses, <u>a great horde, a mighty army. 16 You will advance against my people Israel like a cloud that covers the land</u>. In days to come, Gog, I will bring you against my land, so that the nations may know me when I am proved holy through you before their eyes.

17 '"This is what the Sovereign YHWH says: <u>you are the one I spoke of in former days by my servants the prophets of Israel</u>. At that time they prophesied for years that I would bring you against them. 18 This is what will happen in that day: when Gog attacks the land of Israel, my hot anger will be aroused, declares the Sovereign YHWH. 19 In my zeal and fiery wrath I declare that at that time <u>there shall be a great earthquake in the land of Israel</u>. 20 The fish in the sea, the birds in the sky, the beasts of the field, every creature that moves along the ground, and all the people on the face of the earth will tremble at my presence. The mountains will be overturned, the cliffs will crumble and every wall will fall to the ground. 21 I will summon a sword against Gog on all my mountains, declares the Sovereign YHWH. Every man's sword will be against his brother. 22 I will execute judgment on him with plague and bloodshed; <u>I will pour down torrents of rain, hailstones and burning sulphur on him and on his troops and on the many nations with him</u>. 23 And so I will show my greatness and my holiness, and I will make myself known in the sight of many nations. Then they will know that I am YHWH."

Sounds a bit scary, doesn't it? This passage describes a multitude of nations which will come against Israel. It is not connected to the war we have been describing. There are several clear differences:

First, Israel's situation as described here is quite different from what it is at present. In the *Six Hour War* scenario Israel have neighbours who are '*thorns in their sides*'. That is the present situation – terrorism, BDS, protests against Israel around the world.

Ezekiel describes a very different Israel – *'a land that has recovered from war, whose people were gathered from many nations to the mountains of Israel, which had long been desolate. They had been brought out from the nations, and now all of them live in safety.'*

This describes a scenario several years, at least, after the *Six Hour War*. Israel has recovered from war, the Ingathering – *'from many nations'* – has taken place and *'now all of them live in safety.'* None of this would apply at present.

Secondly, there is no mention of these being surrounding nations – in fact, with the possible exception of Iran (Persia) and a reference to Saudi Arabian towns (Sheba and Dedan, – who are NOT taking part in this attack) – none of the participants in the Psalm 83 war are mentioned. The nations who *are* specifically mentioned – there are many nations who are NOT identified! – are mostly situated at a distance from Israel (the *'far north'* is mentioned) and have no obvious connection to their Arab neighbours – though Islam could well play a part.

Third, the motivation for this attack seems to be greed – NOT the *'everlasting hatred'* which was the motivation for the Psalm 83 attack – *'so that Israel's name is remembered no more.'* Instead, these guys have come *'to loot, to carry off silver and gold, to take away livestock and goods and to seize much plunder.'*

Fourthly, this confederation of nations appears to be led by one man – referred to by Ezekiel as Gog. He appears to be able to raise up many nations to follow him in this enterprise, so a persuasive, charismatic figure. Neither the Psalm 83 war – nor any of the other relevant scriptures – make any mention of an individual at the helm. In fact, the defeat in the *Six Hour War* is partly due to how easily that alliance of nations is divided.

Finally, in the *Six Hour War* Israel are victorious against overwhelming odds – helped, of course, by the fear of YHWH and the disunity of their enemies. In Ezekiel's war, it is YHWH himself – NOT Israel – who will defeat these nations:

Ezekiel 38:22 I will pour down torrents of rain, hailstones and burning sulphur on him and on his troops and on the many nations with him. 23 And so I will show my greatness and my holiness, and I will make myself known in the sight of many nations. Then they will know that I am YHWH.

The subject of this future war in Ezekiel is something I cover in the third book of this series, *Facing the Beast*, but for now let us just absorb the differences that are apparent.

After the *Six Hour War* Israel will become '*a land of unwalled villages ... a peaceful and unsuspecting people – all of them living without walls and without gates and bars ... resettled ruins and the people gathered from the nations, rich in livestock and goods, living at the centre of the earth.*'

In other words Israel will be at peace and no longer seem to have any *'neighbours from hell!'*

The war still to come – summary:

1. The prophet Ezekiel warns of another war against Israel, but the circumstances of this war are very different.

2. He describes a different Israel from what we know today – living securely, at peace and with all the tribes gathered in to Israel.

3. There is no mention of surrounding nations – Arabs are conspicuously absent. Many of these nations come from far away from Israel.

4. The motivation is not the same – greed, instead of the *'ancient hatred'*. They come to loot and plunder Israel's wealth.

5. These nations appear to be led by a charismatic figure. They are united in support of one charismatic leader.

6. It is not Israel who will defeat these nations on this occasion, but YHWH himself – raining down hailstones and burning sulphur upon them.

7. There are no longer any *'neighbours from hell!'*

The End

If you have enjoyed reading this book, perhaps you would take a few minutes to write a short review of it on *Amazon?* Thank you!

If you have not already read the *Six Hours* apocalyptic fiction thriller series you may want to read it next, while the details of this book are still fresh in your mind.

Start with *'In Six Hours … the world changed.'*

You may also enjoy the other non-fiction bible prophecy books by this author:

The Whore and her Mother

the first book in this *Arrows* bible prophecy series:

Oh What Rapture!

and the 3rd book in this *Arrows* bible prophecy series:

Facing The Beast

all available from *Amazon*, etc.

Bibliography

1917: From Palestine to the Land of Israel*
Barry Shaw

A Rabbi Looks at the Last Days
Jonathan Bernis

As America Has Done to Israel*
John P. McTernan

Blood Brothers
Elias Chacour

Britain and Zion
Frank Hardie and Irwin Herrman

Brother Shall Not Lift Sword Against Brother:*
The Roots and Solution to the Problem in the Holy Land
Tzvi Misinai

DNA and Tradition:
The Genetic Link to the Ancient Hebrews*
Rabbi Yaakov Kleiman

Fighting Hamas, BDS and Anti-Semitism
Barry Shaw

God's War on Terror
Walid Shoebat

Guards Without Frontiers:
Israel's War Against Terrorism
Samuel M. Katz

Israel Reclaiming The Narrative: *
Exposing the Big Lie and Its Perpetrators
Barry Shaw

Israel's Lebanon War
Ze'ev Schiff and Ehud Ya'ari

Jews In Places You Never Thought Of*
Karen Primack

Like Dreamers*
Yossi Klein Halevi

O Jerusalem!
Larry Collins and Dominique Lapierre

Operation Babylon
Shlomo Hillel

Phantom Nation:*
Inventing the 'Palestinians' as the Obstacle to Peace – Volume 1
Sha'i ben-Tekoa

Story of My Life
Moshe Dayan

Temple
Bob Cornuke

The Biblical Hebrew Origins of the Japanese People
Joseph Eidelberg

The Claim of Dispossession*
Arieh L. Avneri

The God of the Mountain*
Penny Cox Caldwell

Bibliography

The Igbos: Jews in Africa

Remy Ilona

The Israel Solution:*

A One-State Plan for Peace in the Middle East
Caroline B. Glick

The Jerusalem Temple Mount Myth

Marilyn Sams

The Lonely Soldier*

Adam Harmon

The Temples that Jerusalem Forgot

Ernest L. Martin

We Belong to the Land

Elias Chacour

*Recommended

About the author:

Raymond McCullough, from Co. Down, near Belfast, Northern Ireland, has been a professional writer since 1988, when he authored a regular series – plus other articles, reviews and reports – for several UK computing and publishing magazines.

From 1990-96 he edited and published the Irish magazine, *'Bread'* – releasing his first book, *'Ireland – now the good news!'* from this in 1995; co-edited by his wife, well-known fiction author, Gerry McCullough. His articles have also been published in the *Irish Times*, Dublin, and the *Presbyterian Herald*, Belfast.

In 1993 he hosted a radio show, *'In tha Name a' Gawd!'* on *96.7 BCR*, in Belfast, which later developed into his current radio show of music, news and faith-based interviews – broadcasting around the world on satellite. From 1996, for seven years, he and Gerry led a cell-based Christian fellowship in the Belfast area.

Since then he's been involved in media of all kinds – from web design to podcasting, satellite and internet radio, plus documentary TV production – producing an album of Celtic & Hebrew worship music, *'Into Jerusalem,'* in 2005 and a Celtic pop-folk album, *'Different,'* in 2008.

Raymond researched the subjects in his first bible prophecy book, *'The Whore and her Mother',* for about forty years, off and on, but the events of 9/11 brought a new focus to his research and a real sense of increasing urgency encouraged him to complete that book in just four months!

He felt the subject was too interesting and dramatic to simply be confined to the fairly narrow, evangelical Christian world. He has also recorded a podcast series based on the book, called, *'Fresh Bread: Your Kingdom Come'* – 1-18 & 19-27 – available on *Apple Podcasts (iTunes)*.

Since 2008, Raymond has produced and hosted *'Celtic Roots Radio'* – an *Apple* and *Google* podcast and web station (on *Shoutcast*) – listened to in over 100 countries. He also produces and hosts the *'In tha Name a' Gawd!'* testimony series and *Fresh Bread* – broadcasting each week on satellite. His *'Kingdom Come Trust'* website has hundreds of enthusiastic emails from satellite radio listeners in US, Canada, Australia and the Caribbean.

Raymond has two more bible prophecy books in this *Arrows* series entitled, *'Oh What Rapture!'* and *'Facing the Beast'*. The *Six Hours* series is fiction, but inspired by bible prophecy – *'In Six Hours …the world changed'* and *'In One Hour … Babylon will fall.'* The third book of the trilogy, *'In the Final Hour … the King will return'* is currently under way.

Raymond is also writing a follow-up to *'The Whore and her Mother'* entitled, *'What Kinda People?'* – expanding the contents of his last chapter (WHM) on how we should respond to these prophecies soon to be fulfilled; and is working on a book about Israel, called, *'The Chosen: Israelites, past, present and future'*. He is also working on a TV documentary, filmed mainly in Canada, entitled, *'Broken Treaties.'*

More info at:

www.raymondmccullough.com

www.kingdomcome.org.uk

www.preciousoil.com

www.celticrootsradio.com

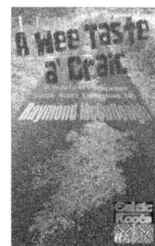

Fiction from Gerry McCullough:

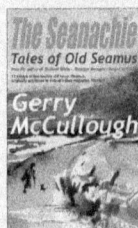

www.ingramcontent.com/pod-product-compliance
Lightning Source LLC
Chambersburg PA
CBHW021131020426
42331CB00005B/719